KU-608-256

YOUR PERSONAL
HOROSCOPE
2019

CANCER

YOUR PERSONAL HOROSCOPE 2019

CANCER

22nd June–22nd July

igloobooks

igloobooks

Published in 2018
by Igloo Books Ltd
Cottage Farm
Sywell
NN6 0BJ
www.igloobooks.com

Copyright © 2018 Foulsham Publishing Ltd

Produced for Igloo Books by Foulsham Publishing Ltd, The Old Barrel Store,
Drayman's Lane, Marlow, Bucks SL7 2FF, England

The Copyright Act prohibits (subject to certain very limited exceptions) the making of copies of
any copyright work or of a substantial part of such a work, including the making of copies by
photocopying or similar process. Written permission to make a copy or copies must therefore
normally be obtained from the publisher in advance. It is advisable also to consult the publisher if
in any doubt as to the legality of any copying which is to be undertaken.

FIR003 0718
2 4 6 8 10 9 7 5 3 1
ISBN: 978-1-78810-499-9

This is an abridged version of material originally published
in Old Moore's Horoscope and Astral Diary.

Cover designed by Nicholas Gage
Edited by Bobby Newlyn-Jones

Printed and manufactured in China

CONTENTS

INTRODUCTION

Your personal horoscopes have been specifically created to allow you to get the most from astrological patterns and the way they have a bearing on not only your zodiac sign, but nuances within it. Using the diary section of the book you can read about the influences and possibilities of each and every day of the year. It will be possible for you to see when you are likely to be cheerful and happy or those times when your nature is in retreat and you will be more circumspect. The diary will help to give you a feel for the specific 'cycles' of astrology and the way they can subtly change your day-to-day life. For example, when you see the sign ☿, this means that the planet Mercury is retrograde at that time. Retrograde means it appears to be running backwards through the zodiac. Such a happening has a significant effect on communication skills, but this is only one small aspect of how the personal horoscope can help you.

With your personal horoscope the story doesn't end with the diary pages. It includes simple ways for you to work out the zodiac sign the Moon occupied at the time of your birth, and what this means for your personality. In addition, if you know the time of day you were born, it is possible to discover your Ascendant, yet another important guide to your personal make-up and potential.

Many readers are interested in relationships and in knowing how well they get on with people of other astrological signs. You might also be interested in the way you appear to very different sorts of individuals. If you are such a person, the section on Venus will be of particular interest. Despite the rapidly changing position of this planet, you can work out your Venus sign, and learn what bearing it will have on your life.

Using your personal horoscope you can travel on one of the most fascinating and rewarding journeys that anyone can take – the journey to a better realisation of self.

THE ESSENCE OF CANCER

Exploring the Personality of Cancer the Crab

(22ND JUNE – 22ND JULY)

What's in a sign?

The most obvious fact about you, particularly when viewed by others, is that you are trustworthy. Sometimes this fact gets on your nerves. Many Cancerians long to be bigger, bolder and more ruthless, but it simply isn't the way you were made. You are basically ruled by your emotions and there is very little you can do to get away from the fact. Once you realise this you could be in for a happy life but there are bound to be some frustrations on the way.

Your ruling planet is the Moon, which changes its position in astrological terms far more quickly than any other heavenly body. That's why you can sometimes feel that you have experienced a whole year's emotions in only a month. However the saving grace of this fact is that unlike the other Water signs of Scorpio and Pisces, you are rarely bogged down by emotional restraints for more than a day or two at a time. This gives you a more optimistic attitude and a determination to use your natural talents to the full, even in the face of some adversity. Caring for others is second nature to you and forms a very large part of your life and character.

Your attitude towards romance fluctuates but is generally of the 'story book' sort. Once you commit yourself to another person, either romantically or practically, you are not likely to change your mind very easily. Loyalty is part of what you are about and doesn't change just because things sometimes get a little complicated. Even when you don't really know where you are going, you are inclined to pull those you love along the path with you, and you can usually rely on their assistance. Basically you are very easy to love and there can't be anything much wrong with that fact. At the same time you can be very practical, don't mind doing some of the dirty work and are in your element when those around you are floundering.

The creative potential within your nature is strong. You are a natural homemaker and tend to get a great deal from simply watching others succeed. All the same this isn't the whole story because you are complex and inclined to be too worrisome.

Cancer resources

Your ruling planet is the Moon, Earth's closest neighbour in space. This means that you are as subject to its tides and fluctuations as is our planet. Of course this is a double-edged sword because you can sometimes be an emotional maelstrom inside. To compensate for this fact you have a level of personal sensitivity that would be admired by many. At the same time you have a deep intuition and can usually be relied upon to see through the mist of everyday life and to work out how situations are likely to mature. This is especially true when it comes to assessing those around you.

As a homemaker you are second to none. You can make a few pounds go a very long way and can cope well in circumstances that would greatly trouble those around you. Adversity is not something that bothers you too much at all and it is clear that you can even revel in difficulty. Nothing is too much trouble when you are dealing with people you love – which includes friends as well as family members.

One of the greatest Cancerian resources is the ability to bring a practical face even to difficult circumstances. Physically speaking you are very resilient, even if you don't always seem to be the strongest person around in an emotional sense. You are given to showing extreme kindness, sometimes even in the face of cruelty from others, though if you are genuinely provoked you can show an anger that would shock most people, even those who think they know you very well indeed.

What really counts the most is your ability to bring others round to your point of view and to get them to do what you think is best. Working from example you won't generally expect others to do anything you are not prepared to try yourself, and your attitude can be an inspiration to others. Through hard work and perseverance you can build a good life for yourself, though your consideration for those around you never diminishes and so even a fortune gained would generally be used on behalf of the world around you. The greatest resource that you possess is your capacity to love and to nurture. This makes you successful and well loved by others.

Beneath the surface

The most difficult aspect of those born under the sign of Cancer the Crab is trying to work out the psychological motivations of this apparently simple but actually deeply complex zodiac position. 'Emotion' is clearly the keyword and is the fountain from which everything, good and bad alike, flows. Whilst some zodiac sign types are inclined to act and then consider the consequences, the Crab is a different beast altogether. The main quality of Cancer is caring. This applies as much to the world at large as it does in consideration of family, though to the Crab it's clear that under almost all circumstances family comes first.

You are a deep thinker and don't always find it easy to explain the way your mind is working. The reason for this is not so difficult to understand. Feelings are not the same as thoughts and it is sometimes quite difficult to express the qualities that rule you internally. What you seem to prefer to do is to put a caring arm around the world and express your inner compassion in this manner. You might also sometimes be a little anxious that if others knew how your innermost mind worked you would become more vulnerable than you already are – which is why the Crab wears a shell in the first place.

At the first sign of emotional pressure from outside you are inclined to retreat into yourself. As a result you don't always confront issues that would be best dealt with immediately. This proclivity runs deep and strong in your nature and can sometimes cause you much more trouble than would be the case if you just made the right statements and asked the correct questions. Physically and mentally you are not inclined to withdraw because you are very much stronger than the world would give you credit for.

Cancerians have a tremendous capacity to love, allied to a potential for positive action when the lives or well-being of others is threatened. In some ways you are the bravest zodiac sign of all because you will march forward into the very gates of hell if you know that you can be of service to those around you. From family to village or town, from town to nation and from nation to a global awareness, yours is the zodiac sign that best epitomises humanity's struggle for a universal understanding.

Making the best of yourself

If you start out from the premise that you are well liked by most people then you are halfway towards any intended destination. Of course you don't always register your popularity and are given to worrying about the impression you give. The picture you paint of yourself is usually very different from the one the world at large sees. If you doubt this, ask some of your best friends to describe your nature and you will be quite surprised. You need to be as open as possible to avoid internalising matters that would be best brought into a more public arena. Your natural tendency to look after everyone else masks a desire to get on in life personally, and the Cancerians who succeed the best are the ones who have somehow managed to bring a sense of balance to their giving and taking.

Try to avoid being too quiet. In social situations you have much to offer, though would rarely do so in a particularly gregarious manner. Nevertheless, and partly because you don't shoot your mouth off all the time, people are willing to listen to what you have to say. Once you realise how strong your influence can be you are already on the road to riches – financial and personal.

Use your imagination to the full because it is one of the most potent weapons in your personal armoury. People won't underestimate you when they know how strong you really are and that means that life can sometimes be less of a struggle. But under most circumstances be your usual warm self, and the love you desire will come your way.

The very practical issues of life are easy for you to deal with, which is why your material success is generally assured. All that is needed to make the picture complete is more confidence in your ability to lead and less inclination to follow.

The impressions you give

There is no doubt at all that you are one of the most loved and the most admired people around. It isn't hard to see why. Your relatives and friends alike feel very protected and loved, which has got to be a good start when it comes to your contacts with the world at large. The most intriguing thing about being a Cancerian subject is how different you appear to be when viewed by others as against the way you judge your own personality. This is down to external appearances as much as anything. For starters you usually wear a cheery smile, even on those occasions when it is clear you are not smiling inside. You give yourself fully to the needs and wants of those around you and are very sympathetic, even towards strangers. It's true that you may not fully exploit the implications of your pleasant nature – but that's only another typical part of your character.

Those people who know you the best are aware that you have a great capacity to worry about things, and they may also understand that you are rarely as confident as you give the external impression of being. They sense the deeply emotional quality of your nature and can observe the long periods of deep thought. When it comes to the practicalities of life, however, you perhaps should not be surprised that you are sometimes put on rather too much. Even this is understandable because you rarely say no and will usually make yourself available when there is work to be done.

True success for the Cancer subject lies in recognising your strong points and in being willing to gain from them in a personal sense. You also need to realise that, to others, the impression you give is what you really are. Bridging the gap between outward calm and inner confusion might be the most important lesson.

The way forward

Although you don't always feel quite as sure of yourself as you give the impression of being, you can still exploit your external appearance to your own and other people's advantage. Your strong sense of commitment to family and your ability to get on well in personal relationships are both factors that improve your ability to progress in life.

Achieving a sense of balance is important. For example you can spend long hours locked into your own thoughts, but this isn't good for you in an exclusive sense. Playing out some of your fantasies in the real world can do you good, even though you are aware that this involves taking chances, something you don't always care to do. At the same time you should not be afraid to make gains as a result of the way you are loved by others. This doesn't come for free and you work long and hard to establish the affection that comes your way.

In practical matters you are capable and well able to get on in life. Money comes your way, not usually as a result of particularly good luck, but because you are a tireless and steady worker. You can accept responsibility, even though the implied management side of things worries you somewhat. To have a career is important because it broadens your outlook and keeps you functioning in the wider world, which is where your personal successes take place. The more you achieve, the greater is the level of confidence that you feel – which in turn leads to even greater progress.

Cancerians should never cut themselves off from the mainstream of life. It's true you have many acquaintances and very few really close friends, but that doesn't matter. Practically everyone you know is pleased to name you as a trusted ally, which has to be the best compliment of all to your apparently serene and settled nature.

In love you are ardent and sincere. It may take you a while to get round to expressing the way you feel, partly because you are a little afraid of failure in this most important area of your life. All the same you love with a passion and are supportive to your partner. Family will always be the most important sphere of life because your zodiac sign rules the astrological fourth house, which is essentially dedicated to home and family matters. If you are contented in this arena it tends to show in other areas of your life too. Your affable nature is your best friend and only tends to disappear if you allow yourself to become too stressed.

CANCER ON THE CUSP

Astrological profiles are altered for those people born at either the beginning or the end of a zodiac sign, or, more properly, on the cusps of a sign. In the case of Cancer this would be on the 22nd of June and for two or three days after, and similarly at the end of the sign, probably from the 20th to the 22nd of July.

The Gemini Cusp – 22nd June to 24th June

You are certainly fun to be around and the sign of Gemini has a great deal to do with your basic motivations. As a result, you tend to be slightly more chatty than the average Cancerian and usually prove to be the life and soul of any party that is going on in your vicinity. Not everyone understands the basic sensitivity that lies below the surface of this rather brash exterior, however, and you can sometimes be a little hurt if people take you absolutely at face value.

There probably isn't the total consistency of emotional responses that one generally expects to find in the Crab when taken alone, and there are times when you might be accused of being rather fickle. All the same, you have a big heart and show genuine concern for anyone in trouble, especially the underdog. Your Gemini attributes give you the opportunity to speak your mind, so when it comes to aiding the world you can be a tireless reformer and show a great ability to think before you speak, which is not typical of Gemini on its own, although there are occasions when the two sides of your nature tend to be at odds with each other.

At work you are very capable and can be relied upon to make instant decisions whenever necessary. Your executive capabilities are pronounced and you are more than capable of thinking on your feet, even if you prefer to mull things over if possible. You are the sort of person that others tend to rely on for advice and will not usually let your colleagues or friends down.

In matters of love, you are less steadfast and loyal than the Crab, yet you care very deeply for your loved ones. People like to have you around and actively seek your advice which, in the main, is considered and sound, though always delivered with humour. You love to travel and would never wish to be limited in either your horizons or your lifestyle. All in all, you are a fun person, good to know, and basically sensible.

The Leo Cusp – 20th July to 22nd July

Here we find a Cancerian who tends to know what he or she wants from life. Part of the natural tendency of the Crab is to be fairly shy and retiring, though progressively less so as the Sun moves on towards the sign of Leo. You are probably aware that you don't exactly match the Cancer stereotype and are likely to be more outspoken, determined and even argumentative at times. You have lofty ideals, which find a ready home for the sensitive qualities that you draw from Cancer. Many social reformers tend to have their Suns very close to the Leo cusp of Cancer and people born on this cusp like to work hard for the world, especially for the less well-off members of society.

In matters of love, you are deep, but ardent and sincere, finding better ways of expressing your emotions verbally than those generally associated with the Crab. You are capable at work, easily able to take on responsibilities that involve controlling other people, and you are outwardly braver than often seems to be the case with Cancer alone. Not everyone finds you particularly easy to understand, probably because there are some definite paradoxes about your nature.

A few problems come along in the area of ideals, which are more important to you than they would be to some of the people with whom you associate. You need to be sure of yourself, a fact that leads to fairly long thinking periods, but once you have formed a particular belief you will move heaven and earth to demonstrate how sensible it is. Don't be too alarmed if not everyone agrees with you.

You are not the typical conformist that might more usually be the case with Cancerians, and feel the need to exercise your civic rights to the full. Tireless when dealing with something you think is especially important, you are a good and loyal friend, a staunch and steadfast lover and you care deeply about your family. However, you are not as confrontational as a person born completely under Leo, and therefore can usually be relied upon to seek a compromise.

CANCER AND ITS ASCENDANTS

The nature of every individual on the planet is composed of the rich variety of zodiac signs and planetary positions that were present at the time of their birth. Your Sun sign, which in your case is Cancer, is one of the many factors when it comes to assessing the unique person you are. Probably the most important consideration, other than your Sun sign, is to establish the zodiac sign that was rising over the eastern horizon at the time that you were born. This is your Ascending or Rising sign. Most popular astrology fails to take account of the Ascendant, and yet its importance remains with you from the very moment of your birth, through every day of your life. The Ascendant is evident in the way you approach the world, and so, when meeting a person for the first time, it is this astrological influence that you are most likely to notice first. Our Ascending sign essentially represents what we appear to be, while the Sun sign is what we feel inside ourselves.

The Ascendant also has the potential for modifying our overall nature. For example, if you were born at a time of day when Cancer was passing over the eastern horizon (this would be around the time of dawn) then you would be classed as a double Cancerian. As such, you would typify this zodiac sign, both internally and in your dealings with others. However, if your Ascendant sign turned out to be a Fire sign, such as Aries, there would be a profound alteration of nature, away from the expected qualities of Cancer.

One of the reasons why popular astrology often ignores the Ascendant is that it has always been rather difficult to establish. We have found a way to make this possible by devising an easy-to-use table, which you will find on page 157 of this book. Using this, you can establish your Ascendant sign at a glance. You will need to know your rough time of birth, then it is simply a case of following the instructions.

For those readers who have no idea of their time of birth it might be worth allowing a good friend, or perhaps your partner, to read through the section that follows this introduction. Someone who deals with you on a regular basis may easily discover your Ascending sign, even though you could have some difficulty establishing it for yourself. A good understanding of this component of your nature is essential if you want to be aware of that 'other person' who is responsible for the way you make contact with the world at large. Your Sun sign, Ascendant sign, and the other pointers in this book will, together, allow you a far better understanding of what makes you tick as an individual. Peeling back the different layers of your astrological make-up can be an enlightening experience, and the Ascendant may represent one of the most important layers of all.

Cancer with Cancer Ascendant

You are one of the most warm and loving individuals that it is possible to know, and you carry a quiet dignity that few would fail to recognise. Getting on with things in your own steady way, you are, nevertheless, capable of great things, simply because you keep going. Even in the face of adversity your steady but relentless pace can be observed, and much of what you do is undertaken on behalf of those you love the most. On the other side of the coin you represent something of a mystery and it is also true that emotionally speaking you tend to be very highly charged. It doesn't take much to bring you to tears and you are inclined to have a special affection for the underdog, which on occasions can get you into a little trouble. Although it is your natural way to keep a low profile, you will speak out loudly if you think that anyone you care for is under attack, and yet you don't show the same tendency on your own behalf.

Rarely if ever out of control, you are the levelling influence everyone feels they need in their life, which is one of the reasons why you are so loved. Your quiet ways are accepted by the world, which is why some people will be astonished when you suddenly announce that you are about to travel overland to Asia. What a great puzzle you can be, but that is half the attraction.

Cancer with Leo Ascendant

This can be a very fortunate combination, for when seen at its best it brings all the concern and the natural caring qualities of Cancer, allied to the more dynamic and very brave face of Leo. Somehow there is a great deal of visible energy here, but it manifests itself in a way that always shows a concern for the world at large. No matter what charitable works are going on in your district it is likely that you will be involved in one way or another, and you relish the cut and thrust of life much more than the retiring side of Cancer would seem to do. You are quite capable of walking alone and don't really need the company of others for large chunks of the average day. However, when you are in social situations you fare very well and can usually be observed with a smile on your face.

Conversationally speaking you have sound, considered opinions and often represent the voice of steady wisdom when faced with a situation that means arbitration. In fact you will often be put in this situation, and there is more than one politician and union representative who shares this undeniably powerful zodiac combination. Like all those associated with the sign of Cancer you love to travel and can make a meal out of your journeys with brave, intrepid Leo lending a hand in both the planning and the doing.

Cancer with Virgo Ascendant

What can this union of zodiac signs bring to the party that isn't there in either Cancer or Virgo alone? Well, quite a bit actually. Virgo can be very fussy on occasions and too careful for its own good. The presence of steady, serene Cancer alters the perspectives and allows a smoother, more flowing individual to greet the world. You are chatty and easy to know, and exhibit a combination of the practical skills of Virgo, together with the deep and penetrating insights that are typical of Cancer. This can make you appear to be very powerful and your insights are second to none. You are a born organiser and love to be where things are happening, even if you are only there to help make the sandwiches or to pour the tea. Invariably your role will be much greater but you don't seek personal acclaim and are a good team player on most occasions.

There is a quiet side to your nature and those who live with you will eventually get used to your need for solitude. This seems strange because Virgo is generally such a chatterbox and, taken on its own, is rarely quiet for long. In matters of love you show great affection and a sense of responsibility that makes you an ideal parent. It is sometimes the case, however, that you care rather more than you should be willing to show.

Cancer with Libra Ascendant

What an absolutely pleasant and approachable sort of person you are, and how much you have to offer. Like most people associated with the sign of Cancer, you give yourself freely to the world and will always be on hand if anyone is in trouble or needs the special touch you can bring to almost any problem. Behaving in this way is the biggest part of what you are and so people come to rely on you very heavily. Like Libra you can see both sides of any coin and you exhibit the Libran tendency to jump about from one foot to the other when it is necessary to make decisions relating to your own life. This is not usually the case when you are dealing with others, however, because the cooler and more detached qualities of Cancer will show through in these circumstances.

It would be fair to say that you do not deal with routines as well as Cancer alone might do and you need a degree of variety in your life. In your case this possibly comes in the form of travel, which can be distant and of long duration. It isn't unusual for people who have this zodiac combination to end up living abroad, though even this does little to prevent you from getting itchy feet from time to time. In relationships you show an original quality that keeps the relationship young, fresh and working well.

Cancer with Scorpio Ascendant

There are few more endearing zodiac combinations than this. Both signs are Watery in nature and show a desire to work on behalf of humanity as a whole. The world sees you as being genuinely caring, full of sympathy for anyone in trouble and always ready to lend a hand when it is needed. You are a loyal friend, a great supporter of the oppressed and a lover of home and family. In a work sense you are capable and command respect from your colleagues, even though this comes about courtesy of your quiet competence, and not as a result of anything that you might happen to say or do.

But we should not get too carried away with external factors, or the way that others see you. Inside you are a boiling pool of emotion. You feel more strongly, love more deeply and hurt more fully than any other combination of the Water signs. Even those who think that they know you really well would get a shock if they could take a stroll around the deeper recesses of your mind. Although these facts are true, they may be rather beside the point because the truth of your passion, commitment and deep convictions may only surface fully half a dozen times in your life. The fact is that you are a very private person at heart and you don't know how to be any other way.

Cancer with Sagittarius Ascendant

You have far more drive, enthusiasm and get-up-and-go than would seem to be the case for Cancer when taken alone, but all of this is tempered with a certain quiet compassion that probably makes you the best sort of Sagittarian too. It's true that you don't like to be on your own or to retire into your shell quite as much as the Crab usually does, though there are, even in your case, occasions when this is going to be necessary. Absolute concentration can sometimes be a problem to you, though this is hardly likely to be the case when you are dealing with matters relating to your home or family, both of which reign supreme in your thinking. Always loving and kind, you are a social animal and enjoy being out there in the real world, expressing the deeper opinions of Cancer much more readily than would often be the case with other combinations relating to the sign of the Crab.

Personality is not lacking, and you tend to be very popular, not least because you are the fountain of good and practical advice. You want to get things done, and retain a practical approach to most situations which is the envy of many of the people you meet. As a parent you are second to none, combining common sense, dignity and a sensible approach. To balance this you stay young enough to understand children.

Cancer with Capricorn Ascendant

The single most important factor here is the practical ability to get things done and to see any task, professional or personal, through to the end. Since half this combination is Cancer, that also means expounding much of your energy on behalf of others. There isn't a charity in the world that would fail to recognise what a potent combination this is when it comes to the very concrete side of offering help and assistance. Many of your ideas hold water and you don't set off on abortive journeys of any kind, simply because you tend to get the ground rules fixed in your mind first.

On a more personal level you can be rather hard to get to know, because both these signs have a deep quality and a tendency to keep things in the dark. The mystery may only serve to encourage people to try and get to know you better. As a result you could attract a host of admirers, many of whom would wish to form romantic attachments. This may prove to be irrelevant, however, because once you give your heart, you tend to be loyal and would only change your mind if you were pushed into doing so. Prolonged periods of inactivity don't do you any good and it is sensible for you to keep on the move, even though your progress in life is measured and very steady.

Cancer with Aquarius Ascendant

The truly original spark, for which the sign of Aquarius is famed, can only enhance the caring qualities of Cancer, and is also inclined to bring the Crab out of its shell to a much greater extent than would be the case with certain other zodiac combinations. Aquarius is a party animal and never arrives without something interesting to say, which is doubly so when the reservoir of emotion and consideration that is Cancer is feeding the tap. Your nature can be rather confusing, even for you to deal with, but you are inspirational, bright, charming and definitely fun to be around.

The Cancer element in your nature means that you care about your home and the people to whom you are related. You are also a good and loyal friend, who would keep attachments for much longer than could be expected for Aquarius alone. You love to travel and can be expected to make many journeys to far-off places during your life. Some attention will have to be paid to your health because you are capable of burning up masses of nervous energy, often without getting the periods of rest and contemplation that are essential to the deeper qualities of the sign of Cancer. Nevertheless you have determination, resilience and a refreshing attitude that lifts the spirits of the people in your vicinity.

Cancer with Pisces Ascendant

A deep, double Water-sign combination, this one, and it might serve to make you a very misunderstood, though undoubtedly popular, individual. You are keen to make a good impression, probably too keen under certain circumstances, and you do everything you can to help others, even if you don't know them very well. It's true that you are deeply sensitive and quite easily brought to tears by the suffering of this most imperfect world that we inhabit. Fatigue can be a problem, though this is nullified to some extent by the fact that you can withdraw completely into the deep recesses of your own mind when it becomes necessary to do so.

You may not be the most gregarious person in the world, simply because it isn't easy for you to put your most important considerations into words. This is easier when you are in the company of people you know and trust, though even trust is a commodity that is difficult for you to find, particularly since you may have been hurt by being too willing to share your thoughts early in life. With age comes wisdom and maturity and the older you are, the better you will learn to handle this potent and demanding combination. You will never go short of either friends or would-be lovers, and may be one of the most magnetic types of both Cancer and Pisces.

Cancer with Aries Ascendant

The main problem that you experience in life shows itself as a direct result of the meshing of these two very different zodiac signs. At heart Aries needs to dominate, whereas Cancer shows a desire to nurture. All too often the result can be a protective arm that is so strong that nobody could possibly get out from under it. Lighten your own load, and that of those you care for, by being willing to sit back and watch others please themselves a little. You might think that you know best, and your heart is clearly in the right place, but try and realise what life can be like when someone is always on hand to tell you that they know better than you do.

But in a way this is a little severe, because you are fairly intuitive and your instincts will rarely lead you astray. Nobody could ask for a better partner or parent than you would be, though they might request a slightly less attentive one. In matters of work you are conscientious, and are probably best suited to a job that means sorting out the kind of mess that humanity is so good at creating. You probably spend your spare time untangling balls of wool, though you are quite sporting too and could even make the Olympics. Once there you would not win however, because you would be too concerned about all the other competitors!

Cancer with Taurus Ascendant

Your main aim in life seems to be to look after everyone and everything that you come across. From your deepest and most enduring human love, right down to the birds in the park, you really do care and you show that natural affection in many different ways. Your nature is sensitive and you are easily moved to tears, though this does not prevent you from pitching in and doing practical things to assist at just about any level. There is a danger that you could stifle those same people whom you set out to assist, and people with this zodiac combination are often unwilling, or unable, to allow their children to grow and leave the nest. More time spent considering what suits you would be no bad thing, but the problem is that you find it almost impossible to imagine any situation that doesn't involve your most basic need, which is to nurture.

You appear not to possess a selfish streak, though it sometimes turns out that in being certain that you understand the needs of the world, you are nevertheless treading on their toes. This eventual realisation can be very painful, but it isn't a stick with which you should beat yourself because at heart you are one of the kindest people imaginable. Your sense of fair play means that you are a quiet social reformer at heart.

Cancer with Gemini Ascendant

Many astrologers would say that this is a happy combination because some of the more flighty qualities of Gemini are somewhat modified by the steady influence of Cancer the Crab. To all intents and purposes you show the friendly and gregarious qualities of Gemini, but there is a thoughtful and even sometimes a serious quality that would not be present in Gemini when taken alone. Looking after people is high on your list of priorities and you do this most of the time. This is made possible because you have greater staying power than Gemini is usually said to possess and you can easily see fairly complicated situations through to their conclusion without becoming bored on the way.

The chances are that you will have many friends and that these people show great concern for your well-being, because you choose them carefully and show them a great deal of consideration. However, you will still be on the receiving end of gossip on occasions, and need to treat such situations with a healthy pinch of salt. Like all part-Geminis your nervous system is not as strong as you would wish to believe and family pressures in particular can put great strain on you. Activities of all kinds take your fancy and many people with this combination are attracted to sailing or wind surfing.

THE MOON AND THE PART IT PLAYS IN YOUR LIFE

In astrology the Moon is probably the single most important heavenly body after the Sun. Its unique position, as partner to the Earth on its journey around the solar system, means that the Moon appears to pass through the signs of the zodiac extremely quickly. The zodiac position of the Moon at the time of your birth plays a great part in personal character and is especially significant in the build-up of your emotional nature.

Your Own Moon Sign

Discovering the position of the Moon at the time of your birth has always been notoriously difficult because tracking the complex zodiac positions of the Moon is not easy. This process has been reduced to three simple stages with our Lunar Tables. A breakdown of the Moon's zodiac positions can be found from page 35 onwards, so that once you know what your Moon Sign is, you can see what part this plays in the overall build-up of your personal character.

If you follow the instructions on the next page you will soon be able to work out exactly what zodiac sign the Moon occupied on the day that you were born and you can then go on to compare the reading for this position with those of your Sun sign and your Ascendant. It is partly the comparison between these three important positions that goes towards making you the unique individual you are.

How To Discover Your Moon Sign

This is a three-stage process. You may need a pen and a piece of paper but if you follow the instructions below the process should only take a minute or so.

STAGE 1 First of all you need to know the Moon Age at the time of your birth. If you look at Moon Table 1, on page 33, you will find all the years between 1921 and 2019 down the left side. Find the year of your birth and then trace across to the right to the month of your birth. Where the two intersect you will find a number. This is the date of the New Moon in the month that you were born. You now need to count forward the number of days between the New Moon and your own birthday. For example, if the New Moon in the month of your birth was shown as being the 6th and you were born on the 20th, your Moon Age Day would be 14. If the New Moon in the month of your birth came after your birthday, you need to count forward from the New Moon in the previous month. Whatever the result, jot this number down so that you do not forget it.

STAGE 2 Take a look at Moon Table 2 on page 34. Down the left hand column look for the date of your birth. Now trace across to the month of your birth. Where the two meet you will find a letter. Copy this letter down alongside your Moon Age Day.

STAGE 3 Moon Table 3 on page 34 will supply you with the zodiac sign the Moon occupied on the day of your birth. Look for your Moon Age Day down the left hand column and then for the letter you found in Stage 2. Where the two converge you will find a zodiac sign and this is the sign occupied by the Moon on the day that you were born.

Your Zodiac Moon Sign Explained

You will find a profile of all zodiac Moon Signs on pages 35 to 38, showing in yet another way how astrology helps to make you into the individual that you are. In each daily entry of the Astral Diary you can find the zodiac position of the Moon for every day of the year. This also allows you to discover your lunar birthdays. Since the Moon passes through all the signs of the zodiac in about a month, you can expect something like twelve lunar birthdays each year. At these times you are likely to be emotionally steady and able to make the sort of decisions that have real, lasting value.

MOON TABLE 1

YEAR	MAY	JUN	JUL	YEAR	MAY	JUN	JUL	YEAR	MAY	JUN	JUL
1921	7	6	5	1954	2	1/30	29	1987	27	26	25
1922	26	25	24	1955	21	20	19	1988	15	14	13
1923	15	14	14	1956	10	8	8	1989	5	3	3
1924	3	2	2/31	1957	29	27	27	1990	24	22	22
1925	22	21	20	1958	18	17	16	1991	13	11	11
1926	11	10	9	1959	7	6	6	1992	2	1/30	29
1927	2/31	29	28	1960	26	24	24	1993	21	19	19
1928	19	18	17	1961	14	13	12	1994	10	8	8
1929	9	7	6	1962	4	2	1/31	1995	29	27	27
1930	28	26	25	1963	23	21	20	1996	18	17	15
1931	17	16	15	1964	11	10	9	1997	6	5	4
1932	5	4	3	1965	1/30	29	28	1998	25	24	23
1933	24	23	22	1966	19	18	17	1999	15	13	13
1934	13	12	11	1967	8	7	7	2000	4	2	1/31
1935	2	1/30	30	1968	27	26	25	2001	23	21	20
1936	20	19	18	1969	15	14	13	2002	12	10	9
1937	10	8	8	1970	6	4	4	2003	1/30	29	28
1938	29	27	27	1971	24	22	22	2004	18	16	16
1939	19	17	16	1972	13	11	11	2005	8	6	6
1940	7	6	5	1973	2	1/30	29	2006	27	26	25
1941	26	24	24	1974	21	20	19	2007	17	17	15
1942	15	13	13	1975	11	9	9	2008	5	4	3
1943	4	2	2	1976	29	27	27	2009	25	23	22
1944	22	20	20	1977	18	16	16	2010	14	12	12
1945	11	10	9	1978	7	5	5	2011	3	2	2
1946	1/30	29	28	1979	26	24	24	2012	20	19	19
1947	19	18	17	1980	14	13	12	2013	10	8	7
1948	9	7	6	1981	4	2	1/31	2014	29	27	25
1949	27	26	25	1982	21	21	20	2015	18	17	16
1950	17	15	15	1983	12	11	10	2016	6	4	4
1951	6	4	4	1984	1/30	29	28	2017	25	24	23
1952	23	22	22	1985	19	18	17	2018	15	13	13
1953	13	11	11	1986	8	7	7	2019	3	2/31	30

TABLE 2   MOON TABLE 3

DAY	JUN	JUL	M/D	O	P	Q	R	S	T	U
1	O	R	0	GE	GE	CA	CA	CA	LE	LE
2	P	R	1	GE	CA	CA	CA	LE	LE	LE
3	P	S	2	CA	CA	CA	LE	LE	LE	VI
4	P	S	3	CA	CA	LE	LE	LE	VI	VI
5	P	S	4	LE	LE	LE	LE	VI	VI	LI
6	P	S	5	LE	LE	VI	VI	VI	LI	LI
7	P	S	6	VI	VI	VI	VI	LI	LI	LI
8	P	S	7	VI	VI	LI	LI	LI	LI	SC
9	P	S	8	VI	VI	LI	LI	LI	SC	SC
10	P	S	9	LI	LI	SC	SC	SC	SC	SA
11	P	S	10	LI	LI	SC	SC	SC	SA	SA
12	Q	S	11	SC	SC	SC	SA	SA	SA	CP
13	Q	T	12	SC	SC	SA	SA	SA	SA	CP
14	Q	T	13	SC	SA	SA	SA	SA	CP	CP
15	Q	T	14	SA	SA	SA	CP	CP	CP	AQ
16	Q	T	15	SA	SA	CP	CP	CP	AQ	AQ
17	Q	T	16	CP	CP	CP	AQ	AQ	AQ	AQ
18	Q	T	17	CP	CP	CP	AQ	AQ	AQ	PI
19	Q	T	18	CP	CP	AQ	AQ	AQ	PI	PI
20	Q	T	19	AQ	AQ	AQ	PI	PI	PI	PI
21	Q	T	20	AQ	AQ	PI	PI	PI	AR	AR
22	R	T	21	AQ	PI	PI	PI	AR	AR	AR
23	R	T	22	PI	PI	PI	AR	AR	AR	TA
24	R	U	23	PI	PI	AR	AR	AR	TA	TA
25	R	U	24	PI	AR	AR	AR	TA	TA	TA
26	R	U	25	AR	AR	TA	TA	TA	GE	GE
27	R	U	26	AR	TA	TA	TA	GE	GE	GE
28	R	U	27	TA	TA	TA	GE	GE	GE	CA
29	R	U	28	TA	TA	GE	GE	GE	CA	CA
30	R	U	29	TA	GE	GE	GE	CA	CA	CA
31	–	U								

AR = Aries, TA = Taurus, GE = Gemini, CA = Cancer, LE = Leo, VI = Virgo,
LI = Libra, SC = Scorpio, SA = Sagittarius, CP = Capricorn, AQ = Aquarius, PI = Pisces

MOON SIGNS

Moon in Aries

You have a strong imagination, courage, determination and a desire to do things in your own way and forge your own path through life.

Originality is a key attribute; you are seldom stuck for ideas although your mind is changeable and you could take the time to focus on individual tasks. Often quick-tempered, you take orders from few people and live life at a fast pace. Avoid health problems by taking regular time out for rest and relaxation.

Emotionally, it is important that you talk to those you are closest to and work out your true feelings. Once you discover that people are there to help, there is less necessity for you to do everything yourself.

Moon in Taurus

The Moon in Taurus gives you a courteous and friendly manner, which means you are likely to have many friends.

The good things in life mean a lot to you, as Taurus is an Earth sign that delights in experiences which please the senses. Hence you are probably a lover of good food and drink, which may in turn mean you need to keep an eye on the bathroom scales, especially as looking good is also important to you.

Emotionally you are fairly stable and you stick by your own standards. Taureans do not respond well to change. Intuition also plays an important part in your life.

Moon in Gemini

You have a warm-hearted character, sympathetic and eager to help others. At times reserved, you can also be articulate and chatty: this is part of the paradox of Gemini, which always brings duplicity to the nature. You are interested in current affairs, have a good intellect, and are good company and likely to have many friends. Most of your friends have a high opinion of you and would be ready to defend you should the need arise. However, this is usually unnecessary, as you are quite capable of defending yourself in any verbal confrontation.

Travel is important to your inquisitive mind and you find intellectual stimulus in mixing with people from different cultures. You also gain much from reading, writing and the arts but you do need plenty of rest and relaxation in order to avoid fatigue.

Moon in Cancer

The Moon in Cancer at the time of birth is a fortunate position as Cancer is the Moon's natural home. This means that the qualities of compassion and understanding given by the Moon are especially enhanced in your nature, and you are friendly and sociable and cope well with emotional pressures. You cherish home and family life, and happily do the domestic tasks. Your surroundings are important to you and you hate squalor and filth. You are likely to have a love of music and poetry.

Your basic character, although at times changeable like the Moon itself, depends on symmetry. You aim to make your surroundings comfortable and harmonious, for yourself and those close to you.

Moon in Leo

The best qualities of the Moon and Leo come together to make you warm-hearted, fair, ambitious and self-confident. With good organisational abilities, you invariably rise to a position of responsibility in your chosen career. This is fortunate as you don't enjoy being an 'also-ran' and would rather be an important part of a small organisation than a menial in a large one.

You should be lucky in love, and happy, provided you put in the effort to make a comfortable home for yourself and those close to you. It is likely that you will have a love of pleasure, sport, music and literature. Life brings you many rewards, most of them as a direct result of your own efforts, although you may be luckier than average and ready to make the best of any situation.

Moon in Virgo

You are endowed with good mental abilities and a keen receptive memory, but you are never ostentatious or pretentious. Naturally quite reserved, you still have many friends, especially of the opposite sex. Marital relationships must be discussed carefully and worked at so that they remain harmonious, as personal attachments can be a problem if you do not give them your full attention.

Talented and persevering, you possess artistic qualities and are a good homemaker. Earning your honours through genuine merit, you work long and hard towards your objectives but show little pride in your achievements. Many short journeys will be undertaken in your life.

Moon in Libra

With the Moon in Libra you are naturally popular and make friends easily. People like you, probably more than you realise, you bring fun to a party and are a natural diplomat. For all its good points, Libra is not the most stable of astrological signs and, as a result, your emotions can be a little unstable too. Therefore, although the Moon in Libra is said to be good for love and marriage, your Sun sign and Rising sign will have an important effect on your emotional and loving qualities.

You must remember to relate to others in your decision-making. Co-operation is crucial because Libra represents the 'balance' of life that can only be achieved through harmonious relationships. Conformity is not easy because Air signs like their independence.

Moon in Scorpio

Some people might call you pushy. In fact, all you really want to do is to live life to the full and protect yourself and your family from the pressures of life. Take care to avoid giving the impression of being sarcastic or impulsive and use your energies wisely and constructively.

You have great courage and you invariably achieve your goals by force of personality and sheer effort. You are fond of mystery and are good at predicting the outcome of situations and events. Travel experiences can be beneficial to you.

You may experience problems if you do not take time to examine your motives in a relationship, and also if you allow jealousy, always a feature of Scorpio, to cloud your judgement.

Moon in Sagittarius

The Moon in Sagittarius helps to make you a generous individual with humanitarian qualities and a kind heart. Restlessness may be intrinsic as your mind is seldom still. Perhaps because of this, you have a need for change that could lead you to several major moves during your adult life. You are not afraid to stand your ground when you know your judgement is right, you speak directly and have good intuition.

At work you are quick, efficient and versatile and so you make an ideal employee. You need work to be intellectually demanding and do not enjoy tedious routines.

In relationships, you anger quickly if faced with stupidity or deception, though you are just as quick to forgive and forget. Emotionally, there are times when your heart rules your head.

Moon in Capricorn

The Moon in Capricorn makes you popular and likely to come into the public eye in some way. The watery Moon is not entirely comfortable in the Earth sign of Capricorn and this may lead to some difficulties in the early years of life. An initial lack of creative ability and indecision must be overcome before the true qualities of patience and perseverance inherent in Capricorn can show through.

You have good administrative ability and are a capable worker, and if you are careful you can accumulate wealth. But you must be cautious and take professional advice in partnerships, as you are open to deception. You may be interested in social or welfare work, which suit your organisational skills and sympathy for others.

Moon in Aquarius

The Moon in Aquarius makes you an active and agreeable person with a friendly, easy-going nature. Sympathetic to the needs of others, you flourish in a laid-back atmosphere. You are broad-minded, fair and open to suggestion, although sometimes you have an unconventional quality which others can find hard to understand.

You are interested in the strange and curious, and in old articles and places. You enjoy trips to these places and gain much from them. Political, scientific and educational work interests you and you might choose a career in science or technology.

Money-wise, you make gains through innovation and concentration and Lunar Aquarians often tackle more than one job at a time. In love you are kind and honest.

Moon in Pisces

You have a kind, sympathetic nature, somewhat retiring at times, but you always take account of others' feelings and help when you can.

Personal relationships may be problematic, but as life goes on you can learn from your experiences and develop a better understanding of yourself and the world around you.

You have a fondness for travel, appreciate beauty and harmony and hate disorder and strife. You may be fond of literature and would make a good writer or speaker yourself. You have a creative imagination and may come across as an incurable romantic. You have strong intuition, maybe bordering on a mediumistic quality, which sets you apart from the mass. You may not be rich in cash terms, but your personal gifts are worth more than gold.

CANCER IN LOVE

Discover how compatible in love you are with people from the same and other signs of the zodiac. Five stars equals a match made in heaven!

Cancer meets Cancer

This match will work because the couple share a mutual understanding. Cancerians are very kind people who also respond well to kindness from others, so a double Cancer match can almost turn into a mutual appreciation society! But this will not lead to selfish hedonism, as the Crab takes in order to give more. There is an impressive physical, emotional and spiritual meeting of minds, which will lead to a successful and inspiring pairing in its own low-key and deeply sensitive way. Star rating: *****

Cancer meets Leo

This relationship will usually be directed by Leo more towards its own needs than Cancer's. However, the Crab will willingly play second fiddle to more progressive and bossy types as it is deeply emotional and naturally supportive. Leo is bright, caring, magnanimous and protective and so, as long as it isn't over-assertive, this could be a good match. On the surface, Cancer appears the more conventional of the two, but Leo will discover, to its delight, that it can be unusual and quirky. Star rating: ****

Cancer meets Virgo

This match has little chance of success, for fairly simple reasons: Cancer's generous affection will be submerged by the Virgoan depths, not because Virgo is uncaring but because it expresses itself so differently. As both signs are naturally quiet, things might become a bit boring. They would be mutually supportive, possibly financially successful and have a very tidy house, but they won't share much sparkle, enthusiasm, risk-taking or passion. If this pair were stranded on a desert island, they might live at different ends of it. Star rating: **

Cancer meets Libra

Almost anyone can get on with Libra, which is one of the most adaptable signs of them all. But being adaptable does not always lead to fulfilment, and a successful match here will require a quiet Libran and a slightly more progressive Cancerian than the norm. Both signs are pleasant, polite and like domestic order, but Libra may find Cancer too emotional and perhaps lacking in vibrancy, while Libra, on the other hand, may be a little too flighty for steady Cancer. Star rating: ***

Cancer meets Scorpio

This match is potentially a great success, a fact which is often a mystery to astrologers. Some feel it is due to the compatibility of the Water element, but it could also come from a mixture of similarity and difference in the personalities. Scorpio is partly ruled by Mars, which gives it a deep, passionate, dominant and powerful side. Cancerians generally like and respect this amalgam, and recognise something there that they would like to adopt themselves. On the other side of the coin, Scorpio needs love and emotional security which Cancer offers generously. Star rating: *****

Cancer meets Sagittarius

Although probably not an immediate success, there is hope for this couple. It's hard to see how this pair could get together, because they have few mutual interests. Sagittarius is always on the go, loves a hectic social life and dances the night away. Cancer prefers the cinema or a concert. But, having met, Cancer will appreciate the Archer's happy and cheerful nature, while Sagittarius finds Cancer alluring and intriguing and, as the saying goes, opposites attract. A long-term relationship would focus on commitment to family, with Cancer leading this area. Star rating: ***

Cancer meets Capricorn

Just about the only thing this pair have in common is the fact that both signs begin with 'Ca'! Some signs of the zodiac are instigators and some are reactors, and both the Crab and the Goat are reactors. Consequently, they both need incentives from their partners but won't find it in each other and, with neither side taking the initiative, there's a spark missing. Cancer and Capricorn do think alike in some ways and so, if they can find their spark or common purpose, they can be as happy as anyone. It's just rather unlikely. Star rating: **

Cancer meets Aquarius

Cancer is often attracted to Aquarius and, as Aquarius is automatically on the side of anyone who fancies it, so there is the potential for something good here. Cancer loves Aquarius' devil-may-care approach to life, but also recognises and seeks to strengthen the basic lack of self-confidence that all Air signs try so hard to keep secret. Both signs are natural travellers and are quite adventurous. Their family life would be unusual, even peculiar, but friends would recognise a caring, sharing household with many different interests shared by people genuinely in love. Star rating: ***

Cancer meets Pisces

This is likely to be a very successful match. Cancer and Pisces are both Water signs, and are both deep, sensitive and very caring. Pisces loves deeply, and Cancer wants to be loved. There will be few fireworks here, and a very quiet house. But that doesn't mean that either love or action is lacking – the latter is just behind closed doors. Family and children are important to both signs and both are prepared to work hard, but Pisces is the more restless of the two and needs the support and security that Cancer offers. Star rating: *****

Cancer meets Aries

A potentially one-sided pairing, it often appears that the Cancerian is brow-beaten by the far more dominant Arian. So much depends on the patience of the Cancerian individual, because if good psychology is present – who knows? But beware, Aries, you may find your partner too passive, and constantly having to take the lead can be wearing – even for you. A prolonged trial period would be advantageous, as the match could easily go either way. When it does work, though, this relationship is usually contented. Star rating: ***

Cancer meets Taurus

This pair will have the tidiest house in the street – every stick of furniture in place, and no errant blade of grass daring to spoil the lawn. But things inside the relationship might not be quite so ship-shape as both signs need, but don't offer, encouragement. There's plenty of affection, but few incentives for mutual progress. This might not prevent material success, but an enduring relationship isn't based on money alone. Passion is essential, and both parties need to realise and aim for that. Star rating: **

Cancer meets Gemini

This is often a very good match. Cancer is a very caring sign and quite adaptable. Geminis are untidy, have butterfly minds and are usually full of a thousand different schemes which Cancerians take in their stride and even relish. They can often be the 'wind beneath the wings' of their Gemini partners. In return, Gemini can eradicate some of the Cancerian emotional insecurity and will be more likely to be faithful in thought, word and deed to Cancer than to almost any other sign. Star rating: ****

VENUS:
THE PLANET OF LOVE

If you look up at the sky around sunset or sunrise you will often see Venus in close attendance to the Sun. It is arguably one of the most beautiful sights of all and there is little wonder that historically it became associated with the goddess of love. But although Venus does play an important part in the way you view love and in the way others see you romantically, this is only one of the spheres of influence that it enjoys in your overall character.

Venus has a part to play in the more cultured side of your life and has much to do with your appreciation of art, literature, music and general creativity. Even the way you look is responsive to the part of the zodiac that Venus occupied at the start of your life, though this fact is also down to your Sun sign and Ascending sign. If, at the time you were born, Venus occupied one of the more gregarious zodiac signs, you will be more likely to wear your heart on your sleeve, as well as to be more attracted to entertainment, social gatherings and good company. If on the other hand Venus occupied a quiet zodiac sign at the time of your birth, you would tend to be more retiring and less willing to shine in public situations.

It's good to know what part the planet Venus plays in your life for it can have a great bearing on the way you appear to the rest of the world and since we all have to mix with others, you can learn to make the very best of what Venus has to offer you.

One of the great complications in the past has always been trying to establish exactly what zodiac position Venus enjoyed when you were born because the planet is notoriously difficult to track. However, we have solved that problem by creating a table that is exclusive to your Sun sign, which you will find on the following page.

Establishing your Venus sign could not be easier. Just look up the year of your birth on the following page and you will see a sign of the zodiac. This was the sign that Venus occupied in the period covered by your sign in that year. If Venus occupied more than one sign during the period, this is indicated by the date on which the sign changed, and the name of the new sign. For instance, if you were born in 1950, Venus was in Taurus until the 27th June, after which time it was in Gemini. If you were born before 27th June your Venus sign is Taurus, if you were born on or after 27th June, your Venus sign is Gemini. Once you have established the position of Venus at the time of your birth, you can then look in the pages which follow to see how this has a bearing on your life as a whole.

1921 TAURUS / 8.7 GEMINI
1922 LEO / 15.7 VIRGO
1923 GEMINI / 10.7 CANCER
1924 CANCER
1925 CANCER / 4.7 LEO
1926 TAURUS / 28.6 GEMINI
1927 LEO / 8.7 VIRGO
1928 GEMINI / 24.6 CANCER /
    18.7 LEO
1929 TAURUS / 8.7 GEMINI
1930 LEO / 15.7 VIRGO
1931 GEMINI / 10.7 CANCER
1932 CANCER
1933 CANCER / 4.7 LEO
1934 TAURUS / 27.6 GEMINI
1935 LEO / 8.7 VIRGO
1936 GEMINI / 24.6 CANCER /
    17.7 LEO
1937 TAURUS / 8.7 GEMINI
1938 LEO / 14.7 VIRGO
1939 GEMINI / 9.7 CANCER
1940 CANCER / 13.7 GEMINI
1941 CANCER / 3.7 LEO
1942 TAURUS / 27.6 GEMINI
1943 LEO / 9.7 VIRGO
1944 GEMINI / 23.6 CANCER /
    17.7 LEO
1945 TAURUS / 7.7 GEMINI
1946 LEO / 14.7 VIRGO
1947 GEMINI / 9.7 CANCER
1948 CANCER / 6.7 GEMINI
1949 CANCER / 2.7 LEO
1950 TAURUS / 27.6 GEMINI
1951 LEO / 9.7 VIRGO
1952 GEMINI / 23.6 CANCER /
    17.7 LEO
1953 TAURUS / 7.7 GEMINI
1954 LEO / 13.7 VIRGO
1955 GEMINI / 8.7 CANCER
1956 CANCER / 29.6 GEMINI
1957 CANCER / 1.7 LEO
1958 TAURUS / 26.6 GEMINI
1959 LEO / 9.7 VIRGO
1960 CANCER / 16.7 LEO
1961 TAURUS / 7.7 GEMINI
1962 LEO / 13.7 VIRGO
1963 GEMINI / 8.7 CANCER
1964 CANCER / 22.6 GEMINI
1965 CANCER / 1.7 LEO
1966 TAURUS / 26.6 GEMINI
1967 LEO / 10.7 VIRGO
1968 CANCER / 16.7 LEO
1969 TAURUS / 6.7 GEMINI
1970 LEO / 13.7 VIRGO
1971 GEMINI / 7.7 CANCER
1972 CANCER / 22.6 GEMINI
1973 CANCER / 30.6 LEO
1974 TAURUS / 26.6 GEMINI /
    22.7 CANCER

1975 LEO / 10.7 VIRGO
1976 CANCER / 15.7 LEO
1977 TAURUS / 6.7 GEMINI
1978 LEO / 12.7 VIRGO
1979 GEMINI / 7.7 CANCER
1980 CANCER / 22.6 GEMINI
1981 CANCER / 30.6 LEO
1982 TAURUS / 26.6 GEMINI /
    21.7 CANCER
1983 LEO / 10.7 VIRGO
1984 CANCER / 15.7 LEO
1985 TAURUS / 6.7 GEMINI
1986 LEO / 12.7 VIRGO
1987 GEMINI / 6.7 CANCER
1988 CANCER / 22.6 GEMINI
1989 CANCER / 29.6 LEO
1990 TAURUS / 25.6 GEMINI /
    20.7 CANCER
1991 LEO / 11.7 VIRGO
1992 CANCER / 14.7 LEO
1993 TAURUS / 5.7 GEMINI
1994 LEO / 11.7 VIRGO
1995 GEMINI / 5.7 CANCER
1996 CANCER / 22.6 GEMINI
1997 CANCER / 29.6 LEO
1998 TAURUS / 25.6 GEMINI /
    20.7 CANCER
1999 LEO / 11.7 VIRGO
2000 CANCER / 14.7 LEO
2001 TAURUS / 5.7 GEMINI
2002 LEO / 11.7 VIRGO
2003 GEMINI / 5.7 CANCER
2004 CANCER / 22.6 GEMINI
2005 CANCER / 29.6 LEO
2006 TAURUS / 25.6 GEMINI /
    20.7 CANCER
2007 LEO / 11.7 VIRGO
2008 CANCER / 14.7 LEO
2009 TAURUS / 5.7 GEMINI
2010 LEO / 11.7 VIRGO
2011 GEMINI / 5.7 CANCER
2012 CANCER / 22.6 GEMINI
2013 TAURUS / 25.6 GEMINI /
    20.7 CANCER
2014 TAURUS / 25.6 GEMINI /
    20.7 CANCER
2015 LEO / 11.7 VIRGO
2016 CANCER / 13.7 LEO
2017 TAURUS / 5.7 GEMINI
2018 LEO / 11.7 VIRGO
2019 GEMINI / 5.7 CANCER

VENUS THROUGH THE ZODIAC SIGNS

Venus in Aries

Amongst other things, the position of Venus in Aries indicates a fondness for travel, music and all creative pursuits. Your nature tends to be affectionate and you would try not to create confusion or difficulty for others if it could be avoided. Many people with this planetary position have a great love of the theatre, and mental stimulation is of the greatest importance. Early romantic attachments are common with Venus in Aries, so it is very important to establish a genuine sense of romantic continuity. Early marriage is not recommended, especially if it is based on sympathy. You may give your heart a little too readily on occasions.

Venus in Taurus

You are capable of very deep feelings and your emotions tend to last for a very long time. This makes you a trusting partner and lover, whose constancy is second to none. In life you are precise and careful and always try to do things the right way. Although this means an ordered life, which you are comfortable with, it can also lead you to be rather too fussy for your own good. Despite your pleasant nature, you are very fixed in your opinions and quite able to speak your mind. Others are attracted to you and historical astrologers always quoted this position of Venus as being very fortunate in terms of marriage. However, if you find yourself involved in a failed relationship, it could take you a long time to trust again.

Venus in Gemini

As with all associations related to Gemini, you tend to be quite versatile, anxious for change and intelligent in your dealings with the world at large. You may gain money from more than one source but you are equally good at spending it. There is an inference here that you are a good communicator, via either the written or the spoken word, and you love to be in the company of interesting people. Always on the look-out for culture, you may also be very fond of music, and love to indulge the curious and cultured side of your nature. In romance you tend to have more than one relationship and could find yourself associated with someone who has previously been a friend or even a distant relative.

Venus in Cancer

You often stay close to home because you are very fond of family and enjoy many of your most treasured moments when you are with those you love. Being naturally sympathetic, you will always do anything you can to support those around you, even people you hardly know at all. This charitable side of your nature is your most noticeable trait and is one of the reasons why others are naturally so fond of you. Being receptive and in some cases even psychic, you can see through to the soul of most of those with whom you come into contact. You may not commence too many romantic attachments but when you do give your heart, it tends to be unconditionally.

Venus in Leo

It must become quickly obvious to almost anyone you meet that you are kind, sympathetic and yet determined enough to stand up for anyone or anything that is truly important to you. Bright and sunny, you warm the world with your natural enthusiasm and would rarely do anything to hurt those around you, or at least not intentionally. In romance you are ardent and sincere, though some may find your style just a little overpowering. Gains come through your contacts with other people and this could be especially true with regard to romance, for love and money often come hand in hand for those who were born with Venus in Leo. People claim to understand you, though you are more complex than you seem.

Venus in Virgo

Your nature could well be fairly quiet no matter what your Sun sign might be, though this fact often manifests itself as an inner peace and would not prevent you from being basically sociable. Some delays and even the odd disappointment in love cannot be ruled out with this planetary position, though it's a fact that you will usually find the happiness you look for in the end. Catapulting yourself into romantic entanglements that you know to be rather ill-advised is not sensible, and it would be better to wait before you committed yourself exclusively to any one person. It is the essence of your nature to serve the world at large and through doing so it is possible that you will attract money at some stage in your life.

Venus in Libra

Venus is very comfortable in Libra and bestows upon those people who have this planetary position a particular sort of kindness that is easy to recognise. This is a very good position for all sorts of friendships and also for romantic attachments that usually bring much joy into your life. Few individuals with Venus in Libra would avoid marriage and since you are capable of great depths of love, it is likely that you will find a contented personal life. You like to mix with people of integrity and intelligence but don't take kindly to scruffy surroundings or work that means getting your hands too dirty. Careful speculation, good business dealings and money through marriage all seem fairly likely.

Venus in Scorpio

You are quite open and tend to spend money quite freely, even on those occasions when you don't have very much. Although your intentions are always good, there are times when you get yourself into the odd scrape and this can be particularly true when it comes to romance, which you may come to late or from a rather unexpected direction. Certainly you have the power to be happy and to make others contented on the way, but you find the odd stumbling block on your journey through life and it could seem that you have to work harder than those around you. As a result of this, you gain a much deeper understanding of the true value of personal happiness than many people ever do, and are likely to achieve true contentment in the end.

Venus in Sagittarius

You are lighthearted, cheerful and always able to see the funny side of any situation. These facts enhance your popularity, which is especially high with members of the opposite sex. You should never have to look too far to find romantic interest in your life, though it is just possible that you might be too willing to commit yourself before you are certain that the person in question is right for you. Part of the problem here extends to other areas of life too. The fact is that you like variety in everything and so can tire of situations that fail to offer it. All the same, if you choose wisely and learn to understand your restless side, then great happiness can be yours.

Venus in Capricorn

The most notable trait that comes from Venus in this position is that it makes you trustworthy and able to take on all sorts of responsibilities in life. People are instinctively fond of you and love you all the more because you are always ready to help those who are in any form of need. Social and business popularity can be yours and there is a magnetic quality to your nature that is particularly attractive in a romantic sense. Anyone who wants a partner for a lover, a spouse and a good friend too would almost certainly look in your direction. Constancy is the hallmark of your nature and unfaithfulness would go right against the grain. You might sometimes be a little too trusting.

Venus in Aquarius

This location of Venus offers a fondness for travel and a desire to try out something new at every possible opportunity. You are extremely easy to get along with and tend to have many friends from varied backgrounds, classes and inclinations. You like to live a distinct sort of life and gain a great deal from moving about, both in a career sense and with regard to your home. It is not out of the question that you could form a romantic attachment to someone who comes from far away or be attracted to a person of a distinctly artistic and original nature. What you cannot stand is jealousy, for you have friends of both sexes and would want to keep things that way.

Venus in Pisces

The first thing people tend to notice about you is your wonderful, warm smile. Being very charitable by nature you will do anything to help others, even if you don't know them well. Much of your life may be spent sorting out situations for other people, but it is very important to feel that you are living for yourself too. In the main, you remain cheerful, and tend to be quite attractive to members of the opposite sex. Where romantic attachments are concerned, you could be drawn to people who are significantly older or younger than yourself or to someone with a unique career or point of view. It might be best for you to avoid marrying whilst you are still very young.

CANCER:
2018 DIARY PAGES

October
2018

1 MONDAY
Moon Age Day 22   Moon Sign Gemini

Socialising would be good today but there may be disputes to deal with. This is because you are very sure of your ground at the moment and you won't be happy if people try to bamboozle you in any way. There are ways and means of getting what you want today and simple confrontation is not one of them.

2 TUESDAY
Moon Age Day 23   Moon Sign Cancer

Events now reach a high watermark because in addition to the lunar high you are also subject to a host of supporting influences. Taken together these indicate that this is the best time to make your move, especially at work. Socially speaking, you will be the very centre of attention making this an extremely interesting day.

3 WEDNESDAY
Moon Age Day 24   Moon Sign Cancer

Expect some changes of direction today and be prepared to act at a moment's notice when opportunities come your way. You should be more filled with energy and determination than has been the case for a while. Good luck is around while the lunar high lasts so make the most of it.

4 THURSDAY
Moon Age Day 25   Moon Sign Leo

Some of your ideas may not find favour with others at this time and you will have to work slightly harder than you have done recently if you want to get the best from even personal situations. It could be that those around you are just being awkward but in some situations they may have a point. Try to be as diplomatic as possible.

5 FRIDAY
Moon Age Day 26   Moon Sign Leo

You can now probably expect to make a significant amount of progress in a practical sense, though you may lose out slightly in the personality stakes. It could be difficult to maintain your popularity with some people in the face of actions you know you should take. Compromises are called for so get your thinking cap on.

6 SATURDAY
Moon Age Day 27   Moon Sign Virgo

You could again be at odds today with someone who doesn't have the same opinions as you do, particularly regarding money and the way it should be either spent or saved. Once again you must rely on your natural diplomacy and turn on the charm in order to get what you want. Not all your decisions now will be easy but they should be honest.

7 SUNDAY
Moon Age Day 28   Moon Sign Virgo

This would be a very good time to put your persuasive tongue to work at home and this makes negotiations or discussions a piece of cake during Sunday. Some of your personal targets in life are now standing on firmer ground than they may have done earlier in the year and all that is required is patience and determination.

8 MONDAY
Moon Age Day 29   Moon Sign Virgo

You remain optimistic and confident at the start of a new working week and you can put many of your present plans into words that those around you will fully understand. Telling a tale is sometimes difficult for you but at the moment you are quite poetic and inclined to sugar any pill.

9 TUESDAY
Moon Age Day 0   Moon Sign Libra

You should now be feeling quite secure about life because although the last month has been busy and eventful it might also have been a little precarious in some ways. It looks as though you can now consolidate some of your schemes and it is also possible that there will be more money around than has recently been the case.

10 WEDNESDAY   *Moon Age Day 1   Moon Sign Libra*

Social interactions see you happily on the go and quite willing to join in with group activities. Rather than being out there alone in the lead you now show a greater tendency to share and to attribute any success you do have to your friends. This may be true in part but don't be so modest that you fail to recognise your own efforts.

11 THURSDAY   *Moon Age Day 2   Moon Sign Scorpio*

Whilst finances should be looking a little rosier you could notice that relationships are causing you one or two problems. The closer people are to you the greater is the chance that they will misbehave or act in ways of which you do not approve. Try to shrug off any little frustrations and don't over-react to them.

12 FRIDAY   *Moon Age Day 3   Moon Sign Scorpio*

Groups and friendship generally are well highlighted, indicating this to be a day that sees you prospering from the involvement of others in your daily life. Stay sociable and out there amidst your friends and don't allow yourself too much time to sit and ruminate. Activity is now the best tonic for the blues.

13 SATURDAY   *Moon Age Day 4   Moon Sign Sagittarius*

Today you are inclined to be somewhat rash, which could lead to difficulties further down the line. Try to be circumspect and to think about eventualities before they actually come along. A little caution is important in your love life because if you make bold statements you may be challenged to back them up in some way.

14 SUNDAY   *Moon Age Day 5   Moon Sign Sagittarius*

A break from your normal routine seems to be indicated on this particular day and is all the more likely if you have the free time to do whatever takes your fancy. You won't want to be doing anything alone at the moment because you are about as sociable as even the friendly Crab gets. Whatever you do, take friends along with you.

15 MONDAY
Moon Age Day 6   Moon Sign Capricorn

There are some inevitable frustrations around while the lunar low pays its monthly visit but these are likely to be fleeting and of no real consequence. Don't take on too much today or tomorrow and give yourself the time you need to rest and relax. Though this might be hard, it would be advantageous.

16 TUESDAY
Moon Age Day 7   Moon Sign Capricorn

Make this a lay off period between adventures and seek the comfort of your own hearth and home if you possibly can. You should be getting on especially well with family members at the moment and your love life should also be a source of great joy. There might not be too much amusement about for the moment.

17 WEDNESDAY
Moon Age Day 8   Moon Sign Capricorn

You tend to be seeing things from the point of view of your family life at the moment and perhaps won't be contributing quite as much as usual out there in the wider world. Real fulfilment presently lies amongst your nearest and dearest but this is likely to be a temporary interlude since outside events demand much more of you by tomorrow.

18 THURSDAY
Moon Age Day 9   Moon Sign Aquarius

The focus is now predominantly on finance and you should find that you have what it takes to attract money – almost without trying. There is unlikely to be a fortune coming your way but little by little there are gains to be made. Strategies made in order to gain more through your work tend to be sound now.

19 FRIDAY
Moon Age Day 10   Moon Sign Aquarius

A fairly lucrative period continues and you should be able to draw more money from places that are fairly surprising. You will also have a strong desire for luxury in one form or another and will want to be in surroundings that are comfortable and pleasing to the eye. Little passes you by today, either at work or home.

20 SATURDAY   *Moon Age Day 11   Moon Sign Pisces*

You may now be inclined to rush in where angels fear to tread and if that means you are doing something that annoys family members, you may be in for a roasting as a result. Bearing in mind how much you hate any sort of fuss or argument, it might still be better to let people do what they want, even if you know they are misguided.

21 SUNDAY   *Moon Age Day 12   Moon Sign Pisces*

Now you really do need to take life one step at a time because if you rush things you are virtually certain to go wrong. Your thinking processes are slightly clouded, perhaps by sentiment, and you need more time to do practically everything. Seek out a little help because there are many people around who are just bursting to lend a hand.

22 MONDAY   *Moon Age Day 13   Moon Sign Pisces*

Continue to look out for new chances and opportunities that are coming your way all the time. If you need financial assistance in order to develop your ideas, think up unique ways to get it. Guard against waste or extravagance because you hate both and won't be happy with yourself if you fail to do so.

23 TUESDAY   *Moon Age Day 14   Moon Sign Aries*

Everyday life keeps you happily on the go and you won't be at all reluctant to push your luck a little when you can see the path ahead clearly. Friends will have a special need of you at present and will rely heavily on your advice and your practical assistance. Putting yourself out for others will be no hardship.

24 WEDNESDAY   *Moon Age Day 15   Moon Sign Aries*

Don't take things to heart on a personal level because there are remarks being made at the moment that are not directed at you, but to which you might attach yourself. Getting hold of the wrong end of the stick is all too easy under present trends but think very carefully before you over-react.

25 THURSDAY · Moon Age Day 16 · Moon Sign Taurus

You remain highly sensitive to your working and living environment and to the moods of other people. Back your hunches all the way because your intuition is as strong as it gets. When it comes to talks or negotiations you can work wonders and will be so tuned-in that you can handle several different situations at the same time.

26 FRIDAY · Moon Age Day 17 · Moon Sign Taurus

Expect some slight setbacks today. They might pass you by unnoticed, but if you do register them it should be easy to address them successfully. Family members can be fractious or difficult to understand and one particular friendship might hit a sticky patch. Just as well that your partner is loving and caring.

27 SATURDAY · Moon Age Day 18 · Moon Sign Gemini

Life for you now means enjoyment and there isn't anyone or anything that can prevent you from having a good time. You are also likely to be extremely creative at the moment and although there is nothing remotely odd about that you can turn your creativity into cash if you think for a while about skills you already possess.

28 SUNDAY · Moon Age Day 19 · Moon Sign Gemini

As long as you keep things organised there are not likely to be any setbacks today. Much depends on your ability to keep a sense of proportion regarding issues that really don't need your involvement. The problem is that a slightly nosey streak is crossing the Crab's path today and you just can't avoid interfering.

29 MONDAY · Moon Age Day 20 · Moon Sign Cancer

You can now capitalise on business and financial investments and could receive unexpected assistance in your efforts to increase your salary. You might receive a surprising gift, though it might be difficult to recognise it as such in the beginning. A sideways look at life perhaps works best for the Crab today.

30 TUESDAY   *Moon Age Day 21   Moon Sign Cancer*

You look and feel strong when going after your objectives but there is just a slight tendency that you could become slightly too confident for your own good. You still need help in some spheres of life and should not turn down the chance of extra support regarding an issue that could be best described as specialised.

31 WEDNESDAY   *Moon Age Day 22   Moon Sign Cancer*

This is a high point for the Crab and a time during which you will demand the attention of the whole world. It might be sensible to start with friends and colleagues, few of whom fail to notice your attractive nature at the moment. You might not feel much like working hard today but you will know how to party.

November
2018

1 THURSDAY
Moon Age Day 23   Moon Sign Leo

Planetary trends now abound with a beneficial focus on finance. You may have the chance to gamble a little but you are unlikely to take the sort of chances that could lead to major difficulties later. Your decisions are likely to be confident and considered and it looks as though others will be very anxious to follow your lead.

2 FRIDAY
Moon Age Day 24   Moon Sign Leo

You should be so dynamic and forceful in your dealings with people generally that some of them may get a shock. It isn't like you to be dominant as you usually get what you want by using your charm. For the moment you will be anxious to cut to the chase in any situation and you won't tolerate what you see as the stupidity of others very well.

3 SATURDAY
Moon Age Day 25   Moon Sign Virgo

Lots of brand new input comes along and your communication skills turn out to be a distinct advantage to you now. Your curiosity knows no bounds and you are willing to go to any lengths to make new discoveries. Some of these might be disquieting but they are also likely to be exciting.

4 SUNDAY
Moon Age Day 26   Moon Sign Virgo

You can now make a strong impact on your surroundings, especially at home. If you have felt slightly uncomfortable with domestic arrangements, now is the time to change them, well ahead of the Christmas period. It could simply be a change in the furniture or else something far more fundamental. Seek other family opinions.

5 MONDAY
Moon Age Day 27   Moon Sign Libra

Today heralds a new and beneficial period, especially when it comes to practical matters. You should be getting on especially well at work and it looks as though you can expect to be considered for advancement or for some sort of honour. This only goes to prove that you have been doing something right over the last few months.

6 TUESDAY
Moon Age Day 28   Moon Sign Libra

You can now afford to be more ambitious and you will have the clout to back up your wishes for the future. In a professional sense you will come as close to being ruthless as the Crab could ever get – but even this is far short of some of the people surrounding you. However you will make an impression and you can forge a new path.

7 WEDNESDAY
Moon Age Day 0   Moon Sign Scorpio

Something you say today is likely to clash with the opinions of people you normally get on with extremely well. The situation cannot be altered but you can realise that people don't always see eye-to-eye and leave it at that. Constantly analysing why individuals say what they do is going to be a real waste of time at the moment.

8 THURSDAY
Moon Age Day 1   Moon Sign Scorpio

You can now be at your intellectual best with sharp insight and an instinctive understanding of how to behave under any given circumstance. Don't expect everyone around you to be equally helpful and try not to be short with people who fail to match your expectations. The Crab's normal patience is sadly missing at present.

9 FRIDAY
Moon Age Day 2   Moon Sign Sagittarius

Quick answers, a great wit and a sense of humour that knows no bounds – all these are gifts that should be evident and even obvious under present trends. You can be quite cutting on occasions and even sarcastic if people cross you. Nobody can doubt that you have an edge and that means people are looking in your direction.

10 SATURDAY   *Moon Age Day 3   Moon Sign Sagittarius*

Involvement with groups is important at this time and you will get on much better with people en masse than you are likely to do with specific individuals. Almost everyone you meet at the moment will have something interesting to tell you and some of the things you learn could be of practical use later on.

11 SUNDAY   *Moon Age Day 4   Moon Sign Sagittarius*

Try as hard as you can to make people understand what you are trying to tell them because the importance of what you are saying is likely to be lost in the complications of life. Even if you have to reinforce your views time and again it will be worth it to get the message across.

12 MONDAY   *Moon Age Day 5   Moon Sign Capricorn*

All of a sudden things are likely to slow to a snail's pace, at least as far as your professional and practical life is concerned. The lunar low can bring you to a virtual standstill but it does nothing to shake your resolve. Instead of actually doing things today and tomorrow, plan your next moves.

13 TUESDAY   *Moon Age Day 6   Moon Sign Capricorn*

Put major issues and decisions on the back-burner and enjoy watching what is happening around you. It is impossible for you to take part in everything, even though you feel as if you should be doing just that. In matters of the heart you prove to be gentle, understanding and willing to listen to an alternative point of view.

14 WEDNESDAY   *Moon Age Day 7   Moon Sign Aquarius*

Test out ideas with regard to their ultimate feasibility before you get yourself too deeply involved in them. Many inventive solutions to old problems are now likely to occur to you and your mind is both ingenious and practical. Not everyone seems to like you at the moment but the people who matter the most certainly will.

15 THURSDAY   *Moon Age Day 8   Moon Sign Aquarius*

You are now extremely powerful when it comes to putting across your point of view but people don't really seem to mind as long as you are fair and open-minded. When you could come unstuck is on those occasions when you dominate conversations or show how dismissive you can be regarding a plan of action that isn't your own.

16 FRIDAY   *Moon Age Day 9   Moon Sign Aquarius*

You are now at your best when you are surrounded by your favourite people, though you may not have that much time for those you don't care for. As a general rule you can cover up your animosity but to do so is more difficult at present. Life is all about attitude and yours can be just a little suspect under present planetary trends.

17 SATURDAY   ☿   *Moon Age Day 10   Moon Sign Pisces*

Your reactions at this time are like lightning and you should be quite happy to put yourself at the forefront of events. Any shyness that might have been present a week or two ago has now disappeared and you have a great sense of purpose and perseverance. Delays early in the day can be quickly overcome.

18 SUNDAY   ☿   *Moon Age Day 11   Moon Sign Pisces*

Not everything you assume to be true turns out to be so and there is a short interlude today that allows you to re-think your strategies and to look at things in a different light. This is a time to back your own hunches, even when others say you are wrong. With perseverance you can easily prove a point today.

19 MONDAY   ☿   *Moon Age Day 12   Moon Sign Aries*

Due to increased enthusiasm you remain energetic, active and willing to take on more and more in the way of responsibility. People you don't see very often might return to your life now and you could also be in touch with someone who lives far away. Routines are boring at present so do something about them.

20 TUESDAY   ☿   *Moon Age Day 13   Moon Sign Aries*

There is some self-deception around at this time and you need to take special care to check things before you proceed in any new direction. There are people who want to be of assistance to you but do they really know what they are doing? In the end you are better off choosing for yourself and staying self-reliant.

21 WEDNESDAY ☿   *Moon Age Day 14   Moon Sign Taurus*

You are enterprising in your outlook and you won't find it difficult to change direction at a moment's notice. This would be a good time to improve yourself in some way – perhaps taking up a new hobby or beginning to study a new subject. The Crab is on a roll and there's no doubting the fact.

22 THURSDAY   ☿   *Moon Age Day 15   Moon Sign Taurus*

An influence comes along right now that is inclined to bring more money into your life. This probably will not come all at once and there won't be any fanfare, but there isn't much doubt that you will be better off in some way soon. Friends prove to be loyal and supportive; on occasions possibly a little too much so.

23 FRIDAY   ☿   *Moon Age Day 16   Moon Sign Taurus*

It could seem difficult to retain control over every single aspect of your life, but do you really need to do so? If you allow other people to do what they think is right for you, you could be quite surprised at the result. Creature comforts could seem more inviting than they have been recently but perhaps this is due to the onset of winter.

24 SATURDAY   ☿   *Moon Age Day 17   Moon Sign Gemini*

With so much forward-looking optimism about, today ought to be something of a dream. There is no doubting your sociable qualities, the planets at the moment see to that, and you are especially entertaining to have around in any social setting. You could be finding new ways to help those who are less well off than you.

25 SUNDAY ☿ *Moon Age Day 18   Moon Sign Gemini*

Your love life is now positively highlighted and this could be the best time of the month for close attachments. You can also enjoy a renaissance in any creative pursuit and everything you do looks both beautiful and seems wise. People generally are crowding in to get your advice because you are such a fair and open individual.

26 MONDAY ☿ *Moon Age Day 19   Moon Sign Cancer*

This is a good time for general progress and a period during which you will be showing yourself off to the best of your ability. You will be very aware of the way you look and the impression you give to others will also be of supreme importance. General good luck and cheer follows you around.

27 TUESDAY ☿ *Moon Age Day 20   Moon Sign Cancer*

The high-energy phase continues as the lunar high works its magic around you. It seems to make others more amenable to your viewpoints, although what is really happening is that you are charming them into accepting your point of view. Romance also looks good and you are likely to be number one in the estimation of someone important.

28 WEDNESDAY ☿ *Moon Age Day 21   Moon Sign Leo*

You can get on well with everyone today – though there's nothing remotely remarkable about that for the average Cancerian. Your confidence remains generally high and your love life in particular should be looking good. You might decide to take a little risk with regard to a particular venture, but proceed with caution as always.

29 THURSDAY ☿ *Moon Age Day 22   Moon Sign Leo*

Don't be at all surprised if there is an element of confusion around today. It isn't that you fail to realise what you should be doing, it's just that things go wrong in more than one way. All of this should be more of a cause for amusement than annoyance, especially as you are in such a happy and positive frame of mind.

30 FRIDAY
☿ *Moon Age Day 23   Moon Sign Virgo*

Certain social acquaintances may prove to be highly useful to your overall path through life at this time. People who you were not particularly close to even a few weeks ago are now playing a much more important part in your life. Keep your eyes and ears open for new input today, no matter what you happen to be doing.

December 2018

1 SATURDAY ☿ *Moon Age Day 24   Moon Sign Virgo*

As you become ever more resourceful, so you start to realise that December could well be the month during which you succeed beyond your previous expectations. A little self-belief is critical to the Crab and you seem to have plenty of it right now. Your creative potential is good and you know how to make things look beautiful.

2 SUNDAY ☿ *Moon Age Day 25   Moon Sign Libra*

This ought to be a day of great inspiration. You really do have a lot going for you at present and there are gains to be made in several different areas of your life. As far as meetings and agreements are concerned today should prove to be inspirational and the only thing you may have to watch out for is the odd awkward friend.

3 MONDAY ☿ *Moon Age Day 26   Moon Sign Libra*

Making an impact on people who are in a position to do you some good has surely never been easier than it is right now. It's time to strike while the iron is hot and to make your feelings known right across the spectrum of your life. People actively want to hear what you have to say and will react positively.

4 TUESDAY ☿ *Moon Age Day 27   Moon Sign Scorpio*

Someone is likely to be relying on your opinions today – in fact a whole variety of people are apt to do so. It might be something as simple as advice about what to buy at the shops or else an issue that is far more serious but whatever you are called upon to comment on today will be important to somebody, so be totally honest.

5 WEDNESDAY ☿ *Moon Age Day 28* *Moon Sign Scorpio*

If you adopt a critical attitude at home, you are in danger of offering unintentional offence. As a rule you tread very carefully around other people's sensibilities but today's trends make you not quite as understanding as would usually be the case. Bite your tongue before you react harshly right now.

6 THURSDAY ☿ *Moon Age Day 29* *Moon Sign Scorpio*

You might decide to do something completely different today and you are likely to have the support of friends who are as bored by convention as you are. Socially speaking you are on top form and the lure of the Christmas season is now fully upon you. Duties will be far less inviting than adventures at this stage.

7 FRIDAY *Moon Age Day 0* *Moon Sign Sagittarius*

Now it pays great dividends to know what your competitors are up to. If you want to get ahead you will need to make it plain what you want from life. Once you have laid your cards on the table you can afford to be slightly more aggressive in going for the prizes that seem to be on offer.

8 SATURDAY *Moon Age Day 1* *Moon Sign Sagittarius*

You may find yourself involved in a domestic situation that amounts to a clash of wills but as the saying goes there is more than one way to skin a cat. Use your very positive communication skills to address tricky issues and persuade others to behave appropriately.

9 SUNDAY *Moon Age Day 2* *Moon Sign Capricorn*

Your energy and vitality are now lower than usual and the lunar low takes the wind from your sails when it comes to practical progress. You may have to be content with half measures or else leave some jobs until later. Making excuses won't please you but in some situations there is very little choice but to do so.

10 MONDAY   *Moon Age Day 3   Moon Sign Capricorn*

Your power is limited and it will be necessary to call upon the good offices of friends and colleagues. There is no shame in this and people will be glad to lend you a hand – particularly bearing in mind how much you do for others. Despite a few attendant problems today you are likely to remain essentially optimistic.

11 TUESDAY   *Moon Age Day 4   Moon Sign Aquarius*

At home it will be better to offer support today than to expect it to be coming your way. People might mean to be helpful but what actually happens is that they make a few small problems worse. You remain very dependable and your nearest and dearest will recognise this. Accept that there might not be much time to spend on yourself.

12 WEDNESDAY   *Moon Age Day 5   Moon Sign Aquarius*

Leave some space for the emotions of those around you. Although you might think you feel strongly about certain issues there are other people who are far more emotionally stretched than you. Your caring and understanding nature is a great part of your personality and this really does need to show today.

13 THURSDAY   *Moon Age Day 6   Moon Sign Aquarius*

A more enriched period now makes itself felt. It won't be what happens on the surface that is most interesting at the moment but rather the undertones of life. Almost every person you meet feels they are an expert in one thing or another and this fact alone means you might have to sort out a number of tortured issues.

14 FRIDAY   *Moon Age Day 7   Moon Sign Pisces*

It should now be quite easy to express your emotions. This is a good time to clear the air and to say something that has been on your mind for quite a while. As December grows older and the winter weather makes itself known, you could easily be inclined to seek out a warm fireside and the company of family members.

15 SATURDAY
Moon Age Day 8   Moon Sign Pisces

This can be a period of improved relationships and communication with friends. This weekend you will happily sally forth and look for new situations and different kinds of mental stimulation. Your attitude becomes more expansive and you begin to wake up to some exciting new possibilities tied to the season.

16 SUNDAY
Moon Age Day 9   Moon Sign Pisces

Your domestic affairs enter a more expansive phase at this time. It could be that you are making changes ahead of Christmas or simply looking for a new way of living your life. The changes probably won't be radical but they do count and should help you to feel better about the time of year and more content with your lot.

17 MONDAY
Moon Age Day 10   Moon Sign Aries

Dealings with some other people might seem fairly unsatisfactory, mainly because you can't get them to do exactly what you would wish. There is also a good deal of uncertainty in your mind under present trends and a tendency to do things time and again, even though you know in your heart they were fine before.

18 TUESDAY
Moon Age Day 11   Moon Sign Aries

Activities today tend to be more fun than serious and any truly honest assessment of your life at this time should show you to be generally content with your lot. Of course there are always things you want that you don't have but many of these will come in good time. Don't get too tied to pointless routines today.

19 WEDNESDAY
Moon Age Day 12   Moon Sign Taurus

This would be a very good time to benefit from the diversity of interests that are so typical of your nature under present trends. With more energy at your disposal and the chance to put it to good use, you will find yourself tackling all manner of new jobs. People turn to you for help and advice at the moment, which you are pleased and qualified to offer.

20 THURSDAY
Moon Age Day 13   Moon Sign Taurus

Take things steadily and don't overestimate your capacity for work today. Although you have plenty of energy throughout the month, this may not be specifically the case today. Pace yourself and allow others to take some of the strain. If you go to bed tonight feeling absolutely drained, you may still feel fatigued tomorrow.

21 FRIDAY
Moon Age Day 14   Moon Sign Gemini

This is a day that could be marked by a distinct lack of discipline in practical affairs. In some ways you prefer to let things ride, rather than pitching in and sorting them out once and for all. Your attitudes could be slightly unrealistic and you may need to talk to someone who has more age or experience than you.

22 SATURDAY
Moon Age Day 15   Moon Sign Gemini

If you are slightly quieter today you can be fairly sure that this is a very temporary state of affairs, brought about by the position of the Moon. It's true you will be thinking things through carefully and you may not be quite as gregarious as you have been recently. All of this changes tomorrow when you throw caution to the wind.

23 SUNDAY
Moon Age Day 16   Moon Sign Cancer

The Moon moves into Cancer and that means you will have the lunar high coming along at the very end of the year. Social impulses are as strong as ever and you should have sufficient energy to move around freely and to involve yourself in life. Make the most of this.

24 MONDAY
Moon Age Day 17   Moon Sign Cancer

Important changes you want to make at home now become more of a reality and you are definitely in a good position to influence the thinking of people who can be quite intransigent on occasions. Good fortune is on your side and makes for a potentially good and fulfilling Christmas Eve.

25 TUESDAY *Moon Age Day 18   Moon Sign Leo*

Christmas Day for Cancer should be great and you may enjoy fruitful encounters with a number of different people today, some of whom are offering the sort of information that is both timely and useful. Where love and romance are concerned, it is not difficult to find the right words to sweep someone off their feet during the festivities.

26 WEDNESDAY *Moon Age Day 19   Moon Sign Leo*

It appears that personal and intimate matters bring out the best in you for Boxing Day. Concentrating on the family, rather than distant friends or even work, certainly seems to appeal. If you find yourself facing a mountain of tasks, the best approach is to break them down into easily manageable units and do them one at a time.

27 THURSDAY *Moon Age Day 20   Moon Sign Virgo*

There's no doubt about it. You have plenty of new ideas today, even if actually putting them into practice isn't all that easy, what with the holiday period and the necessities of the season. Nevertheless, there is nothing to prevent you from looking at future strategies, and playing one or two of them through in your mind.

28 FRIDAY *Moon Age Day 21   Moon Sign Virgo*

Today should find you on top form and eager for almost anything that comes along. It's true that you won't be good at working, but the holiday season is in full swing and the Crab loves to have fun. Some family members may be feeling suitably nostalgic now and you are no exception.

29 SATURDAY *Moon Age Day 22   Moon Sign Libra*

Perhaps you feel slightly restricted because you need to mix with as many different sorts of people today as proves to be possible. At the back of your mind are a number of different ideas, some of which involve innovation. There are individuals appearing now who will listen to what you have to say and who may even offer to help.

30 SUNDAY
Moon Age Day 23   Moon Sign Libra

Keep your ears open because what you learn in group situations today could prove to be extremely useful in the end. Listen to what is being said but don't commit yourself to joining in unless you are very sure of your ground. You are likely to be awash with energy today and quite willing to take on more than is good for you.

31 MONDAY
Moon Age Day 24   Moon Sign Libra

You might enter the last day of the year with a little extra seriousness, though not for long. Of course you will want to work out what you have and have not achieved across the last twelve months and also to plan ahead. However, most of what today should be about is enjoying yourself and making things great for everyone around you.

CANCER:
2019 DIARY PAGES

CANCER:
YOUR YEAR IN BRIEF

Start as you mean to go on – that's the best adage for Cancer this year. January and February offer all sorts of new opportunities for growth and development. The weather might be cold but this year at least you don't mind that at all. Routines can hold you back but determination will see you through. There are gains to be made from following up on promising leads.

People you don't see very often are likely to be turning up during March and April, and you could also make some new friends. Keep ringing the changes whenever it is possible to do so because for the Crab right now variety really is the spice of life. Romance is likely to be high on your agenda during April, at a time when you are waking up to the possibilities of spring.

The late spring will be quite delightful for most Cancerians. You will be at your most charming and well able to get others to do your bidding simply by asking. Money matters should be easier to deal with and both May and June bring you closer to achieving longed-for objectives, especially at work or in regard to new interests. In a competitive mood, you may be taking up new activities that test you more than usual.

Along comes the summer and both July and August should find you raring to go and anxious to do anything necessary to get out and about and to travel, perhaps to some exotic places. Despite a busy time you are likely to be quite reflective and wistful, which can sometimes be the way of the Crab. This is the sensitive side of your nature that everyone is longing to see and which lifts your popularity amongst your friends and family.

As the days shorten and autumn arrives you remain pretty much in charge of your life. You won't give up responsibilities you have worked hard for and you should also find that family commitments take on greater significance. You may have an urge to travel and you certainly will not settle for second best in business, social matters or love. People who come into your life at this time may have an important part to play in the months and years ahead.

The last two months of the year, November and December, will see you making still greater advances towards some of your chosen objectives. With plenty to play for in the career stakes, you remain very much aware that it is your own effort that counts. The Christmas period will find you full of beans and anxious to make everyone as happy as you should be feeling yourself. With this positive mood could come some amazing surprises.

January

2019

1 TUESDAY
Moon Age Day 25   Moon Sign Scorpio

A private matter might need your personal attention early on New Year's Day, but otherwise you should be more than willing to share your thoughts and feelings with those around you. The Crab begins the year in an open and honest frame of mind and you could be quite surprised by the reaction to your present honesty.

2 WEDNESDAY
Moon Age Day 26   Moon Sign Scorpio

A minor boost to your present finances could come along any time now. You should find yourself able to mix and mingle with some fairly useful people and it is just possible you are taking a slightly more selfish attitude to life generally. This isn't a common situation for Cancer but it may well be justified now.

3 THURSDAY
Moon Age Day 27   Moon Sign Sagittarius

There may be some conflict regarding financial issues, perhaps due to a little extravagance on your part at some stage in the past. This is an issue that you should be able to deal with quite easily and you are unlikely to allow it to get in the way of achieving any personal goals around this time.

4 FRIDAY
Moon Age Day 28   Moon Sign Sagittarius

Present planetary influences bring out the very best in you where communication is concerned. It's true that you are not the most talkative person in the world as a rule but all that changes under today's astrological trends. You have it about you to influence the decision making of some important people.

5 SATURDAY   *Moon Age Day 0   Moon Sign Capricorn*

Prepare to feel somewhat frustrated as far as some of your ambitions are concerned as only patience will get you where you want to be. This quality may not be so easy to find at the moment, so it will be necessary to limit yourself to situations you know and understand. The new and unusual can wait.

6 SUNDAY   *Moon Age Day 1   Moon Sign Capricorn*

A source of irritation could arise from your finances making it necessary to look carefully at expenditure. This is not to say you are without cash but you probably cannot afford to spend lavishly on goods and services that are unnecessary. A continuing reliance on specific friends is also possible.

7 MONDAY   *Moon Age Day 2   Moon Sign Capricorn*

There is no point in worrying about situations you cannot control. Of course this is easy to say but it really is true that you can't influence everything. Leave some matters to others and also be willing to accept a little help when it is offered. The people around you may turn out to be quite generous now.

8 TUESDAY   *Moon Age Day 3   Moon Sign Aquarius*

Your desire for success and a little impetuosity can be of great use to you at this time. Although you may not be looking directly at the practical or financial side of life, the people you meet and their personalities may lead to benefits in that area that you did not expect.

9 WEDNESDAY   *Moon Age Day 4   Moon Sign Aquarius*

There are almost certain to be significant ups and downs in the workplace today, while the more personal side of your life looks likely to be smooth and steady. As a result there is a natural tendency to turn your attention towards house and home. The Crab may retreat a little around this time.

10 THURSDAY
Moon Age Day 5   Moon Sign Pisces

Now you may find it easier to advance yourself at work, mainly as a result of the continued effort you have been putting in and because the general planetary trends are looking more favourable. Rules and regulations might seem to be an irritant but it should be possible to rise above them.

11 FRIDAY
Moon Age Day 6   Moon Sign Pisces

Trends once again positively highlight communication in your chart, so it seems likely that you will be taking in just as much information as you can. Chatty and interested, you appear bright and happy to the people around you. Your zodiac sign in this frame of mind is capable of just about anything and certainly makes an impression.

12 SATURDAY
Moon Age Day 7   Moon Sign Pisces

Look out for the possibility of some domestic changes right now and embrace them if you know they are going to work in your best interests eventually. You could find yourself working hard on two separate fronts and if this is the case, you will need a good deal of energy to make gains under these trends.

13 SUNDAY
Moon Age Day 8   Moon Sign Aries

It is clear that you know how to get the best from others around this time and you can really feather your nest by taking note of the reactions that are coming your way and by modifying your own attitude accordingly. There might be something just slightly sneaky about you right now but it can pay off.

14 MONDAY
Moon Age Day 9   Moon Sign Aries

You can get the absolute maximum from all home-based efforts and associations this week. This might not be the best time of the year to think about travel but you are likely to be quite happy with your lot. A shopping spree may be possible but you won't want to go too far or stay out too long.

15 TUESDAY　　　*Moon Age Day 10　Moon Sign Taurus*

Today finds you in a good state of mind to get any amount of jobs done in and around your home. Your sensitivity to the needs of others and the insight you are showing generally are quite noteworthy. Don't take too much notice of family members who are rather dramatic at present.

16 WEDNESDAY　　*Moon Age Day 11　Moon Sign Taurus*

Someone close to you has an important message to impart at the moment and it would not be sensible to ignore it. All the same, there simply isn't time to listen to everything that is being said because you are likely to find yourself involved in what amounts to an extremely busy day.

17 THURSDAY　　　*Moon Age Day 12　Moon Sign Taurus*

Events at work could turn out to be more than profitable and will offer you the chance to look at responsibilities in an entirely different way. Don't rush your fences because slow and steady wins just about any race at the moment. Romance could prove very interesting by the end of the day.

18 FRIDAY　　　　*Moon Age Day 13　Moon Sign Gemini*

Standard responses probably won't work at the moment and it is very important to be original, especially when dealing with colleagues and superiors. It is fortunate that you have the gift of the gab right now because this will offer you a response for every occasion. It is your intelligence that others really notice now.

19 SATURDAY　　　*Moon Age Day 14　Moon Sign Gemini*

Personal matters have more going for them than career issues at present. The response that comes from loved ones, especially your partner, ought to find you very happy with your lot. If there are any frustrations around at the moment, these are likely to come from colleagues or friends who are behaving strangely.

20 SUNDAY
Moon Age Day 15   Moon Sign Cancer

Personal success is more than possible at this time, partly due to your resilient attitude and willingness to go on working when others are tired. It could be that people in authority are watching you very closely and so the fact that you are shining right now certainly works to your advantage.

21 MONDAY
Moon Age Day 16   Moon Sign Cancer

Good luck is never far away now that the Moon is in your own zodiac sign bringing with it the time of the month known as the lunar high. Keep up your efforts to get ahead because these are aided by some quite positive influences astrologically. Having fun has rarely been easier and you will be particularly carried away by the attention that surrounds you socially.

22 TUESDAY
Moon Age Day 17   Moon Sign Leo

A very practical attitude slowly begins to prevail and you now have both feet in the real world, probably for the first time for a number of days. You should find it easy to act on impulse and this might pay dividends. Routines will bore you and there is a good chance that you will overturn an issue that has annoyed you for a while.

23 WEDNESDAY
Moon Age Day 18   Moon Sign Leo

If you have it in your mind to bring a personal issue to a head, you could well have chosen the wrong day to do it. There are some matters that will put themselves right if you only remain patient. Meanwhile, you need to be having a good time. A little trip out to somewhere interesting might prove fortuitous.

24 THURSDAY
Moon Age Day 19 · Moon Sign Virgo

An increase in the general level of your luck might seem to indicate that this would be the best time for a little gamble, but don't be fooled. In a few days you might be able to take one or two cautious chances but for the moment hold on to what you have, especially in terms of money. Listen out for interesting conversations that are taking place around now.

25 FRIDAY
Moon Age Day 20   Moon Sign Virgo

You really do want to be noticed at the moment and this may be obvious both in the way you dress and in the manner you use to address people. Superiors will be looking favourably at you but you don't have to do anything special to attract their attention. In practical matters slow and steady wins the race.

26 SATURDAY
Moon Age Day 21   Moon Sign Libra

There seems to be no reason why plans and schemes should not proceed in a very satisfactory way. The only slight stumbling block might be your determination to get some change into your life. This means that a particular task you had earmarked for today may have to wait until you are feeling more settled.

27 SUNDAY
Moon Age Day 22   Moon Sign Libra

Trends now place a lively accent on potentially important meetings and should see you offering your considered opinion whenever it is sought. Friends ought to be demanding a good deal of your time but they do have your best interests at heart. Avoid getting involved in a family disagreement that is not of your making.

28 MONDAY
Moon Age Day 23   Moon Sign Scorpio

You will probably be pretty much on the go from morning until night because there are things to do and you are in a very practical frame of mind. The extra tasks you take on won't bother you in the slightest because you have plenty of energy in reserve. By the evening you might decide to socialise with friends.

29 TUESDAY
Moon Age Day 24   Moon Sign Scorpio

A pleasing family matter is likely to leave you feeling contented now and this ought to be a warm and happy sort of day for most Cancerians. It should not be difficult to conform to an expected pattern and taking the line of least resistance seems to be more appealing at present than might sometimes be the case.

30 WEDNESDAY *Moon Age Day 25   Moon Sign Sagittarius*

Attracting the right sort of attention should be a piece of cake right now and you maintain a very positive attitude towards life in general. Trends suggest that someone you don't see all that often could make a return visit to your life now and might bring with them some exciting new possibilities.

31 THURSDAY *Moon Age Day 26   Moon Sign Sagittarius*

It might seem early in the day as if certain strengths within your character that you take for granted are now somehow lacking. How wrong you are! When the chips are down you prove to be a reliable friend and to have all the answers you need in any situation. Trust your own judgement and don't allow yourself to be diverted from a path you know is right.

February
2019

1 FRIDAY
Moon Age Day 27   Moon Sign Sagittarius

Although this isn't the best time to start tackling your big ambitions you can spend time thinking about them a great deal, and in doing so should lay down some hard and fast plans. To some extent you will want to remain in your own little world but that is something that is crucially important for the Crab from time to time.

2 SATURDAY
Moon Age Day 28   Moon Sign Capricorn

The lunar low demands that you spend time looking at life, rather than involving yourself in it too much. Spare a thought for those who are less well off than you are and take time out to lend them a hand. You might as well, because your own practical progress is slowed to something like a standstill.

3 SUNDAY
Moon Age Day 29   Moon Sign Capricorn

Don't push yourself too hard right now. Allow others to make some of the running while you decide how you can best clear the decks for action later. Your confidence should return towards the end of the day, when you may choose to socialise more and might be pushing for a somewhat exciting evening.

4 MONDAY
Moon Age Day 0   Moon Sign Aquarius

There is a tendency for you to assume that you know your own opinion without thinking about it. This could be something of a mistake because it is clear that you are quite perceptive. When it comes to assessing the way another person is likely to behave, you should be second to none. Listen to what your intuition tells you.

5 TUESDAY
Moon Age Day 1   Moon Sign Aquarius

It might seem that domestic partners have your best interests at heart, but that doesn't necessarily mean that you will be happy with what they are doing. There is just the chance that you are being a little illogical at the moment and you might benefit from standing back and taking stock.

6 WEDNESDAY
Moon Age Day 2   Moon Sign Aquarius

Be aware that some financial fluctuations might come along, but you could make the most of them to elicit financial gains. You are very astute at present and would not be likely to falter over important decisions. Planetary trends insist that you spend at least part of the day considering your nearest and dearest.

7 THURSDAY
Moon Age Day 3   Moon Sign Pisces

You display an extremely quick wit and a great ability to communicate well. Your creative potential is also extremely good and you won't be stuck for an idea when it comes to changes in and around your home. Where practical necessities are concerned, get these out of the way early and leave yourself more time for enjoyment later.

8 FRIDAY
Moon Age Day 4   Moon Sign Pisces

A generally busy and quite involved social period seems likely both now and across the weekend. You won't forget how important it is to concentrate on the matter in hand but you will be sought out continually for the sort of advice that your zodiac sign is so good at offering. Accept advice when it is offered.

9 SATURDAY
Moon Age Day 5   Moon Sign Aries

If there is anything specific on your mind right now, enlist the support of friends, one or two of whom may be ready to make themselves available to you. There might be less cash about than seemed to be the case recently but present interests don't depend so much on money. Most of your enjoyment comes from elsewhere.

10 SUNDAY   *Moon Age Day 6   Moon Sign Aries*

You may not have to work too hard to get by financially. Planetary trends seem to indicate that what you need more or less automatically comes your way as and when you need it. Some of this could be as a result of assistance from others. Also, the Crab is even more affectionate than usual at this time.

11 MONDAY   *Moon Age Day 7   Moon Sign Aries*

Though you are now entering an especially rewarding phase, this is not a day to believe absolutely everything you hear. At least one person might be trying to fool you in some way so use your intuition when assessing the motives of those with whom you come into contact.

12 TUESDAY   *Moon Age Day 8   Moon Sign Taurus*

You are in a mood for personal enjoyment and can appreciate your own better qualities more than would usually be the case. Don't be held back by irrelevant details and stick to your mainline plans. There is a strong chance you are being singled out for special treatment by someone you rate highly.

13 WEDNESDAY   *Moon Age Day 9   Moon Sign Taurus*

Some issues are almost certain to irritate you today and it is essential for you to ignore what might appear to be insults from people close to you. In all probability you are too sensitive for your own good, which is a personality trait of the sign of Cancer. Try to be reasonable in your attitude and don't take offence without good cause.

14 THURSDAY   *Moon Age Day 10   Moon Sign Gemini*

The support of those you love matters the most now, which is quite appropriate on Valentine's Day! Meanwhile, seeking approval from the world in general is far less important. You focus on your own personal contentment, and practical success becomes somewhat less important. Routines can also feel quite comfortable around now.

15 FRIDAY
Moon Age Day 11   Moon Sign Gemini

Today should be quite favourable for adventure or any sort of travel. Although there are slight setbacks to be dealt with from time to time, in the main you find that you can make significant progress. Don't be too quick to take the word of a stranger over that of a friend, even if you are at first convinced.

16 SATURDAY
Moon Age Day 12   Moon Sign Cancer

The lunar high brings a very positive period to this part of the month, and might show that you are somewhat better off than you expected. You will know instinctively how to make money and should be filled with excellent ideas. Stand by to make a romantic conquest at some time around now.

17 SUNDAY
Moon Age Day 13   Moon Sign Cancer

Lucky influences abound and all you have to do is to register their presence in your life. Fortune favours direct actions and you shouldn't hold back when you instinctively know that something is right. It's time to take the bull by the horns, especially so in personal matters.

18 MONDAY
Moon Age Day 14   Moon Sign Leo

You seem to be the life and soul of any party that is taking place around you right now, even if some of them are arranged at very short notice. Give yourself a pat on the back for a recent job well done but don't stand still. It's time to move on in one way or another so keep up the effort.

19 TUESDAY
Moon Age Day 15   Moon Sign Leo

Present trends have the ability to bring you out of your shell and offer a chance to mix with people who could have a profound bearing on your life. Practical matters are now easy to deal with but you may feel that there is a little something missing from more personal attachments.

20 WEDNESDAY   *Moon Age Day 16   Moon Sign Virgo*

Social activities again take centre stage today, partly at least because it will be difficult to get ahead in other ways. Practical jobs are likely to remain undone and you will need to show a good deal of patience when dealing with wayward family members. This is a day during which you should keep yourself busy.

21 THURSDAY   *Moon Age Day 17   Moon Sign Virgo*

Objectives that are now on the drawing board need looking at very carefully before you commit yourself in any way. Your confidence is fairly high right now but you could be inclined to fire from the hip, not a good thing to do at the moment. Take your time and discuss things with people who are in the know.

22 FRIDAY   *Moon Age Day 18   Moon Sign Libra*

This is a great day for assessing your own position and situation in life generally. You are likely to be attentive to details but less inclined to dominate others with your own ideas. The more sensitive side of your nature is now on display and you also appreciate the quieter aspects of life.

23 SATURDAY   *Moon Age Day 19   Moon Sign Libra*

Someone you know well might have some pretty startling news to give you. There are potential gains to be made on the financial front and very few people are likely to stand in your way around this time. Concentrate your efforts with regard to a family issue and make sure you listen to what your nearest and dearest are really saying.

24 SUNDAY   *Moon Age Day 20   Moon Sign Scorpio*

Once again, be on the lookout for new social contacts and make the most of what life has to offer you. Not everyone will be on your side, but when it matters the most you should be able to make some headway. Avoid getting involved in pointless disputes at work or petty arguments with family members.

25 MONDAY *Moon Age Day 21   Moon Sign Scorpio*

Today should be given over to the things that most appeal to you and you won't be too concerned with the more practical aspects of life. You may get the chance to make some small financial gains, though these are likely to come along by chance rather than as a result of your own direct planning.

26 TUESDAY *Moon Age Day 22   Moon Sign Sagittarius*

Now you can balance times when you honestly want to withdraw into yourself with those times when you need to interact with others. You may struggle to find your confidence, but if you rely on the support that comes from your loved ones, you should manage well enough.

27 WEDNESDAY *Moon Age Day 23   Moon Sign Sagittarius*

Don't waste your time on trivialities today. You should be quite keen to focus on the most important matters for you, even if you are regularly interrupted by situations that are of no real importance. The start of a new month is close and holds a glimmer of optimism with regard to a job issue that has been on your mind for a while.

28 THURSDAY *Moon Age Day 24   Moon Sign Sagittarius*

Someone or something in your day-to-day life may occupy your thoughts at the moment and even lead you to become quite obsessive about it. Try to focus on getting on with other matters to take your mind off it, and the less the problem should concern you. Take time to relax, even though that might be rather difficult under prevailing circumstances.

March

2019

1 FRIDAY
Moon Age Day 25   Moon Sign Capricorn

There is a distinct possibility of disagreements in the workplace today. The lunar low can slightly take the wind out of your sails and trends suggest that you will need to be sure of your ground before you start insisting you are right about things. If at all possible, spend the day relaxing.

2 SATURDAY
Moon Age Day 26   Moon Sign Capricorn

This would be a very good time to exercise caution in most of your dealings and indeed it might be best to do as little as possible for the moment. Keep life straight and easy and don't get involved in situations you don't understand. Don't be tempted to act on impulse until later in the day.

3 SUNDAY
Moon Age Day 27   Moon Sign Aquarius

Now your light tends to shine more brightly and you are keen to impress others with your personality. There is little to hold you back at present and you should have plenty of enthusiasm for new projects. Family members will be especially warm and loving now, though you will want to spend time with new friends too.

4 MONDAY
Moon Age Day 28   Moon Sign Aquarius

It really would be best to listen to those around you now and not to take their advice for granted. Although your own intuition is usually quite reliable this isn't quite so likely to be the case at the moment. If you follow the opinions of someone who really cares for you, you might avoid an embarrassing situation.

5 TUESDAY *Moon Age Day 29   Moon Sign Aquarius*

There is likely to be a desire to get things done as quickly as you can but make sure you avoid too much impetuosity. The steadier you take things, the greater the likelihood you will get them right first time. In a social sense, you should start making arrangements now to ensure that next weekend turns out well.

6 WEDNESDAY ☿ *Moon Age Day 0   Moon Sign Pisces*

Some sort of emotional release is likely to be on the cards and at the same time your business acumen is good. There are gains to be made from acting quickly, whilst other people are still thinking about things. This would be particularly true in any sort of auction or a purchase that requires immediate action.

7 THURSDAY ☿ *Moon Age Day 1   Moon Sign Pisces*

You will value your independence highly at the moment and you won't willingly relinquish it. You are likely to enjoy getting away from routines and will not be tremendously committed to any at present. The weekend is only a day or two away and it should turn out to be more exciting than any for a few weeks.

8 FRIDAY ☿ *Moon Age Day 2   Moon Sign Aries*

With emotions quite close to the surface, now is the time to be telling your partner just how wonderful they are. Today has all the potential excitement of yesterday, but also has great warmth. There are gains to be made through small investments and even through the odd carefully calculated gamble.

9 SATURDAY ☿ *Moon Age Day 3   Moon Sign Aries*

Don't be surprised if you find yourself in the limelight. People really notice you at present and some of them may find it necessary to put you on a pedestal. Whether or not you find this position particularly comfortable remains to be seen but it might be best to make the most of the situation.

10 SUNDAY ☿ *Moon Age Day 4   Moon Sign Taurus*

Your natural kindness is amplified today, at a time when it seems natural to be doing all you can for others. Standing up for friends who can't defend themselves is second nature to you, and you now have a great desire to go one step further in your need to be of use. Routines could appear tedious today.

11 MONDAY ☿ *Moon Age Day 5   Moon Sign Taurus*

You relish challenges at present and won't be held back by situations you might once have thought to be beyond your own control. Friends ought to be extremely helpful but you may spend as much time putting right things they have done for you than you would if you had done them for yourself.

12 TUESDAY ☿ *Moon Age Day 6   Moon Sign Taurus*

You can be your own worst critic at the moment. This is a little unfortunate because there are people around who will take you at your word. Set out to give the impression that you are capable of almost anything, and this in turn should instil confidence in those with whom you mix and ensure their support.

13 WEDNESDAY ☿ *Moon Age Day 7   Moon Sign Gemini*

You may opt for fairly easy chores today, not because you fail to be successful but on account of a great ability to get others to do things for you. Is this lazy? Perhaps, but it seems as though everyone wants to lend a hand and it might be churlish to refuse them the chance. Interludes for personal space come later in the day.

14 THURSDAY ☿ *Moon Age Day 8   Moon Sign Gemini*

Your intellect is honed to perfection now and the decisions you make are based upon the clarity of insight you have into certain situations. Career moves you might make at this time are likely to be fortunate and this is not a period during which you will have to do anything twice.

15 FRIDAY ☿ *Moon Age Day 9   Moon Sign Cancer*

You can make a success of almost anything today. Supported strongly by the presence of the lunar high, you are exciting, happy and keen to be on the move. The fact that this trend coincides with the end of the working week proves to be doubly fortunate. Progress should be easy to make.

16 SATURDAY ☿ *Moon Age Day 10   Moon Sign Cancer*

Making important progress with new opportunities is now as easy as pie. Lady Luck should be shining her light on you and there are also gains to be made in a personal sense. This might not be the most enjoyable day of the year so far but it certainly isn't far away from proving to be so for many Crabs.

17 SUNDAY ☿ *Moon Age Day 11   Moon Sign Cancer*

You have a great desire to get about socially and when it comes to speaking your mind you are second to none at the moment. The attitude of friends is very positive and they tend to back you up when you need it the most. A particular job that might have been quite demanding could be nearly finished.

18 MONDAY ☿ *Moon Age Day 12   Moon Sign Leo*

There might be a slight testing of your patience today, most likely as a result of work and the way colleagues or superiors seem to be taking you for granted. It would be better not to react too strongly but rather to show how sweet you can be. Some extra forbearance now pays dividends further down the line.

19 TUESDAY ☿ *Moon Age Day 13   Moon Sign Leo*

There is great personal strength on display right now, together with a sort of regal quality in your nature that others notice almost immediately. Although you might think you are not the flavour of the month with certain individuals, nothing could be further from the truth, as you should soon discover.

20 WEDNESDAY ☿   *Moon Age Day 14   Moon Sign Virgo*

A few minor disagreements might have to be overcome before you can get your own way today. All the same, you might be forced to ask yourself whether if you have to put in so much effort, the end product is worth it? Only you can decide. By the evening a more romantic quality should ensue.

21 THURSDAY ☿   *Moon Age Day 15   Moon Sign Virgo*

Revitalise your personal life whenever you can. Make sure you are first when it comes to handing out compliments in a romantic sense and put new zest into an old attachment if you get the chance. There isn't a great deal to be done professionally today, so you may as well concentrate on things closer to home.

22 FRIDAY ☿   *Moon Age Day 16   Moon Sign Libra*

Problems and obstacles don't look easy to overcome today but don't worry because things are going to look very different over the weekend. Simply do what you have to and as far as work is concerned clear the decks for action that comes early next week. There is a sort of quiet optimism around if you look for it.

23 SATURDAY ☿   *Moon Age Day 17   Moon Sign Libra*

Good trends come along at just the right time to offer you a crackerjack of a weekend. Put mindless or boring tasks on hold and settle for having a good time instead. You can certainly enjoy yourself now in almost any sort of company though old friends will probably suit you the best.

24 SUNDAY ☿   *Moon Age Day 18   Moon Sign Scorpio*

Life on the whole ought to feel fairly stable today but there is a tinge of potential excitement that simply will not go away. It might take you a while to wake up to new opportunities but once you do, nothing prevents you from exploring them. There is an almost pathological need at present to be loved and to know that you are.

25 MONDAY ☿ *Moon Age Day 19* *Moon Sign Scorpio*

If someone offers you a challenge today, your reaction could be that of a bull to a red rag. In a strongly competitive mood, you will not want to turn away from any test. However, trends suggest that you should fight this natural instinct today and that you really have nothing to prove but lots to lose if you get your response wrong.

26 TUESDAY ☿ *Moon Age Day 20* *Moon Sign Sagittarius*

You remain ambitious, even if you are turning just a little introspective in some ways. The year is advancing fast and it would be really good today to spend some time out of doors, appreciating what the spring has to offer. If you combine this with time spent in the company of your partner or sweetheart, so much the better.

27 WEDNESDAY ☿ *Moon Age Day 21* *Moon Sign Sagittarius*

You will need to be fully in touch with others in order to get on well at the moment. Try not to go it alone too much and be willing to accept a point of view that might not be your own if you know intuitively that it has merit. Someone you love quite deeply can be a little thoughtless at present but don't react too strongly to this.

28 THURSDAY ☿ *Moon Age Day 22* *Moon Sign Capricorn*

The lunar low is inclined to take you by surprise somewhat and may also lead to delays or cancellations where appointments are concerned. Acting on impulse is not to be recommended today or tomorrow and you are likely to be far better off simply following the line of least resistance.

29 FRIDAY *Moon Age Day 23* *Moon Sign Capricorn*

A steady day is likely and also most useful right now. Do what you have to do and even enjoy the possibility of routines that might sometimes bore you. Don't get involved in disagreements at home and be willing to spend an hour or two on your own because the quieter qualities of Cancer are now quite marked in your chart.

30 SATURDAY   *Moon Age Day 24*   *Moon Sign Capricorn*

A lot of your energy now goes into making something work out the way you would wish in a career sense, or with regard to education. Cancer is very creative at this time and you might be taking on board new interests that have a special appeal. Trends suggest that mechanical objects might let you down somewhat at this time.

31 SUNDAY   *Moon Age Day 25*   *Moon Sign Aquarius*

It looks as though you will encounter the odd or unusual quite a lot at the moment. This is no problem at all for Cancer because such things are meat and drink to your sometimes unusual nature. Try to stay away from the dark side of your mind today. It has no place at present and can restrict forward movement when it really matters.

April

2019

1 MONDAY
Moon Age Day 26   Moon Sign Aquarius

You are more than able to use your imagination in practical ways at present and can have a lot of fun on the way. However, not everyone understands the unusual way your mind sometimes works and, as this can be a time of practical jokes for some Crabs, make sure you don't end up being the April Fool!

2 TUESDAY
Moon Age Day 27   Moon Sign Pisces

It could be that the necessities of your career are putting a real strain on your home-life, or it might be the case that you simply are not taking as much notice of those you love as you probably should. Make sure you reverse the trend now by spending more time in their company and by being especially kind.

3 WEDNESDAY
Moon Age Day 28   Moon Sign Pisces

There are strong signposts to success around at the moment but you have to search hard to see some of them. Maybe you will be looking back for lessons that the past taught you and that can be a good thing, just as long as you bear in mind that present circumstances are likely to be rather different.

4 THURSDAY
Moon Age Day 29   Moon Sign Pisces

This is an ideal period for reorganisation and for spring-cleaning generally. It doesn't really matter if this is at work or home or whether it is of the practical or the mental sort. What does count right now is that you are willing to admit that not everything is quite what it might be. As the week grows older, so you get more energetic.

5 FRIDAY *Moon Age Day 0   Moon Sign Aries*

At work you are able to put your alert mind to use and you are quite capable of thinking on your feet. You possess great common sense and an ability to see situations in a way that others cannot. Socially speaking, your personality shines out and you are very good at attracting new friends.

6 SATURDAY *Moon Age Day 1   Moon Sign Aries*

Relationships and romantic matters generally have the power to bring out the best in you around this time. Your confidence is boosted by the way those around you are heaping on the compliments but it is probably no more than you rightfully deserve. Your creative potential remains especially good during this weekend.

7 SUNDAY *Moon Age Day 2   Moon Sign Taurus*

At home you tend to be quite forceful and will expect your opinions to be taken on board but present trends show that you are likely to be far less dominant out in the wide world beyond your door. Cancer does have its quiet side and this seems to be showing for a day or two.

8 MONDAY *Moon Age Day 3   Moon Sign Taurus*

You get along especially well with friends, and this trend can also be turned into an interesting time with regard to business. People are willing to help you now and this applies just as much to commercial matters as it does to personal ones. This might be an opportune time to push your luck a little.

9 TUESDAY *Moon Age Day 4   Moon Sign Gemini*

As a direct reversal to some of the trends that have been around for the last few days, you may now feel yourself to be just slightly isolated. This need not turn out to be a bad thing, on the contrary you can use it to your advantage. You are very adaptable and thoughtful at this time.

10 WEDNESDAY   *Moon Age Day 5   Moon Sign Gemini*

You show yourself as being extremely moderate in your opinions and ideas now and, working on the positive trends that surround you, it is possible to make a very good impression on others. You are embarking on a search to find ever better ways of expressing yourself, especially to strangers.

11 THURSDAY   *Moon Age Day 6   Moon Sign Gemini*

You find a great deal in the way of goodwill coming from people who matter quite a lot. Don't be afraid to use this to achieve objectives you might have only dreamed about in the past. It looks as though you will be in good company, at a time when the social side of life proves to be very important.

12 FRIDAY   *Moon Age Day 7   Moon Sign Cancer*

A time of self-determination comes along and you will almost certainly have more personal confidence today and tomorrow than at any other time during April. That's why this is the time to grab the bull by the horns. Cancerians who are working today should really make significant progress.

13 SATURDAY   *Moon Age Day 8   Moon Sign Cancer*

As you are especially outgoing today, you will want to make the best impression you can, particularly when you are meeting people for the very first time. Your confidence keeps rising and you should find that even those people who have crossed you in the past are much less likely to do so now.

14 SUNDAY   *Moon Age Day 9   Moon Sign Leo*

You can look forward to a rapidly expanding circle of social contacts in the days that lie ahead, a trend that should already be making itself known this Sunday. The odd financial gain isn't out of the question but most of the importance in this weekend comes from your desire to simply have a good time.

15 MONDAY
Moon Age Day 10   Moon Sign Leo

You could receive a useful boost from relatives and friends, even if this is only a series of compliments that make you believe in yourself much more than usual. Romance is highlighted at present but it is possible that not all the personal attention coming your way is from the direction you would expect.

16 TUESDAY
Moon Age Day 11   Moon Sign Virgo

There is a great deal to be had today through teamwork and general co-operation with others. With a lot to gain from taking on new projects you should be quite energetic and anxious to help out anywhere when you can. Some unusual circumstances could surround aspects of your love life later in the day.

17 WEDNESDAY
Moon Age Day 12   Moon Sign Virgo

Although probably not exactly the luckiest day of the month, things should tend to fall into place fairly well today. The difference is that what comes your way is now generally as a result of your own efforts and not restricted to chance happenings. Trends indicate that you might be sought out for your specific expertise.

18 THURSDAY
Moon Age Day 13   Moon Sign Libra

When it comes to personal objectives, things happen today that put you fully in the picture. Watch out because you could be slightly accident-prone and might end up doing certain jobs more than once in order to get them right. Use that good Cancerian intuition in order to work out how best to react.

19 FRIDAY
Moon Age Day 14   Moon Sign Libra

Things are still looking pretty good in a practical sense. Attitude is important when getting on at work and you won't have things all your own way in any sphere of life. Accommodation and understanding is the key, particularly if you are dealing with younger family members who insist on being awkward.

20 SATURDAY   *Moon Age Day 15   Moon Sign Scorpio*

A little daydreaming is no problem and is actually quite essential to the Cancerian nature. Don't push any issue for today but be willing to watch and wait. By tomorrow everything is likely to change and so there isn't too much sense in rushing your fences for the moment. Friends should be very accommodating.

21 SUNDAY   *Moon Age Day 16   Moon Sign Scorpio*

A break from everyday routines would probably suit you best on this particular day. You can't keep your mind focused on practical issues all the time and would certainly gain from pleasing yourself a little more at this time. If you don't have to work today you might enjoy a shopping spree.

22 MONDAY   *Moon Age Day 17   Moon Sign Sagittarius*

Busy professional trends come and go in the week ahead, leaving you with more time to get on with things that suit you personally. Although you may experience significant interruptions, you have it within you to keep your eye on the ball. One thing you find it difficult to avoid now is gossip, which is likely to prove quite diverting.

23 TUESDAY   *Moon Age Day 18   Moon Sign Sagittarius*

Although there can be a little tension about at the moment it isn't you who is causing it. Don't get involved in disputes that rightfully have nothing to do with you and although Cancer often plays the peacemaker, to try to do so at the moment might only lead to you being disliked by one party or another.

24 WEDNESDAY   *Moon Age Day 19   Moon Sign Capricorn*

This is a time for keeping things simple. The lunar low need not have too much of a bearing on your life this month, just as long as you don't strive for the impossible. Keep your demands, both of yourself and others, reasonably limited and accept that you are going to have failures as well as successes.

25 THURSDAY   *Moon Age Day 20*   *Moon Sign Capricorn*

Events might seem to conspire against you at this stage of the working week and this will be especially noticeable if you are a working Crab. Be willing to listen to some sound and sensible advice and don't be too keen to overturn obstacles, even those that look easy. There is time enough for that later.

26 FRIDAY   *Moon Age Day 21*   *Moon Sign Capricorn*

Today could seem like an island of fun. You certainly won't want to concentrate solely on the same old boring routines and will have all the energy you need to get ahead yourself and to persuade others to come along. Seek out somewhere particularly interesting, even if it means travelling somewhere.

27 SATURDAY   *Moon Age Day 22*   *Moon Sign Aquarius*

Messages are coming along at the moment and you should pay attention to them. The only problem might be that they appear in the strangest places. The odd, the unusual and the peculiar all have a part to play in your day and all conspire to make this one of the weirdest yet most fascinating times of the month.

28 SUNDAY   *Moon Age Day 23*   *Moon Sign Aquarius*

This Sunday almost inevitably brings a need for change and a desire to push the pedal to the metal in a social sense. Mix as freely as you can with as many different sorts of people as come your way. You should have a lot of patience when it comes to dealing with friends who are presently having difficulties.

29 MONDAY   *Moon Age Day 24*   *Moon Sign Pisces*

It isn't likely to be existing friends that stand out today but rather newcomers in your life. Cancerians tend to have very few close friends but a new one could definitely be made around now. All aspects related to outdoor matters, such as gardening for example, will have a real appeal at the moment.

30 TUESDAY
Moon Age Day 25   Moon Sign Pisces

Your intuition is honed to perfection right now, so when it comes to assessing the potential in people or situations, you should have no difficulty at all. Whatever the weather is doing at the moment you can gain significantly from getting some fresh air and from being in stimulating and even exciting company.

May

2019

1 WEDNESDAY
Moon Age Day 26   Moon Sign Pisces

Today brings close emotional attachments very much to the fore. On exactly the other side of the coin your sporting incentive is also very strong. Splitting yourself between the needs and desires of today is not going to be at all easy but if you plan carefully all should be well.

2 THURSDAY
Moon Age Day 27   Moon Sign Aries

Though the outer world has some challenges to offer, you might prefer to stay with what you know. That doesn't mean you are going to sit around and watch the grass grow but does infer that quieter pursuits would suit you better than a riotous time. Stick to friends you know well and trust implicitly.

3 FRIDAY
Moon Age Day 28   Moon Sign Aries

If you want to get into the good books of others, this is the day to do it. A combination of excellent perception, together with an ability to get on side with just about anyone, makes this the time to ask for what you want. Some Crabs might even achieve an increase in salary around now.

4 SATURDAY
Moon Age Day 0   Moon Sign Taurus

You seem to have the secret of popularity at the moment because even without trying you are making a good impression. Actually you are quite a magnetic person and you are probably the only one who doesn't realise this fact. Switch on your mystical charm in order to turn a few heads.

5 SUNDAY
Moon Age Day 1   Moon Sign Taurus

This is a time during which you actively want to reach out socially and to make a good impression. You might decide to take on some new educational interest or to display your creative abilities more than might have been possible in the recent past. A very good period for new starts.

6 MONDAY
Moon Age Day 2   Moon Sign Taurus

You are likely to find that the necessary energy to break new ground effectively is missing, just when you need it the most. There are ways round this slight inconvenience. Get others to work on your behalf, whilst you supervise. Someone you thought disliked you could be proving the exact opposite later today.

7 TUESDAY
Moon Age Day 3   Moon Sign Gemini

Today might just bring a few surprises and at a time when they can really pep up your life. You can't take anything for granted at the moment and should be willing to go with the flow, especially in a social sense. The better you react to changing circumstances, the greater are the rewards that will come your way.

8 WEDNESDAY
Moon Age Day 4   Moon Sign Gemini

There are some points to be scored today, both at work and in a more personal sense. With plenty to play for and people quite willing in the main to follow your lead, there is no reason to hang back. Once work is out of the way you will want to turn your mind to something particularly different.

9 THURSDAY
Moon Age Day 5   Moon Sign Cancer

Decision-making is easy for you now, and this is the time of the month during which you can make up your mind quickly and decisively. There are likely to be some gifts coming your way, even though some of these may turn out to be very different from expected. Keep a cool head when it matters the most.

10 FRIDAY
Moon Age Day 6   Moon Sign Cancer

Life continues to be generally good for you and it's worth pushing your luck this Friday. The Moon is still on your side and it offers you plenty of incentives, both financial and personal. If you want to make an especially good impression socially, put on that new outfit and really paint the town red.

11 SATURDAY
Moon Age Day 7   Moon Sign Leo

You can benefit from finding yourself in the middle of a day that is far less demanding than some of the ones you have experienced of late. Today would be fine for all those little domestic chores that have been piling up and you will also find moments to spend with your partner or family members.

12 SUNDAY
Moon Age Day 8   Moon Sign Leo

You are now well equipped to make friends and influence people, even if the incentive to do so isn't quite as strong today as it was recently. In addition to your personable streak, there is also a very private Cancerian in evidence. The combination might be difficult for some people to understand.

13 MONDAY
Moon Age Day 9   Moon Sign Virgo

You are out to show the world that you know what you are talking about but it's very important that you know this is genuinely the case. Check all details and make this a time to undertake some very necessary research. Keeping up with the Jones's isn't something that is as important to you now as it is to those with whom you live.

14 TUESDAY
Moon Age Day 10   Moon Sign Virgo

Your power to make things go how you want them to is temporarily diminished but you need to be certain in your mind that this is not a situation that is going to last long. This is a time to think and to clear the decks for new action in the days ahead. You may actively choose to spend time in solitary contemplation.

15 WEDNESDAY   *Moon Age Day 11   Moon Sign Libra*

Your dealings with others are likely to contain more than a few pleasant encounters and this looks like being a generally happy sort of day. Don't hog the limelight at work because there is someone who desperately needs to shine. Your generosity now will stand you in good stead later.

16 THURSDAY   *Moon Age Day 12   Moon Sign Libra*

What really stands out now is your ability to say exactly the right thing at the right time. There are people around who will be queuing up to be in your gang at present and Cancer has rarely shone brighter. The only slight fly in the ointment might be the need to look closely at finances.

17 FRIDAY   *Moon Age Day 13   Moon Sign Scorpio*

The need for your personal input on a certain issue is clearly paramount at present so don't hold back when it comes to putting forward your point of view. You may be expected to take the lead in some new projects and though you might find yourself a little nervous, in the end you are almost certain to come good.

18 SATURDAY   *Moon Age Day 14   Moon Sign Scorpio*

Don't be put off by obstacles this weekend because they won't get in your way. It's true that some situations look potentially troublesome but once you roll up your sleeves and pitch in, nothing could be further from the truth. You have the ability to turn drudgery into pleasure today.

19 SUNDAY   *Moon Age Day 15   Moon Sign Scorpio*

You can use this period in order to rise well to certain challenges and there isn't anything preventing you from putting in that extra bit of effort that really counts. If it seems that nothing particularly exciting is happening at present the reason could be that you aren't putting in enough input.

20 MONDAY *Moon Age Day 16   Moon Sign Sagittarius*

A period of renewal and regeneration is at hand but don't expect quite the level of activity that has been the case of late. You are thinking deeply about things and will be more than happy to spend a few hours on your own if that's what it takes to get the best results. Be patient over financial issues.

21 TUESDAY *Moon Age Day 17   Moon Sign Sagittarius*

Communication once again proves to be your main area of satisfaction, as has been the case for some time. You won't be short of very good ideas, but putting them into practice won't be quite as easy as you might have wished. You should feel confident to speak your mind when it really counts at work.

22 WEDNESDAY *Moon Age Day 18   Moon Sign Capricorn*

Today is a real patience tester and you can blame the lunar low for this. Don't allow yourself to become annoyed at people who seem determined to misunderstand you. As long as you retain your sense of humour and your ability to see things in your unique perspective, awkward trends won't last.

23 THURSDAY *Moon Age Day 19   Moon Sign Capricorn*

You need to know when you are beaten, if only so you can start thinking along different lines. There's no point whatsoever in flogging a dead horse and you might need to tell friends that this is the case. In many respects you are happy to be a loner at present and won't want anyone telling you what to do.

24 FRIDAY *Moon Age Day 20   Moon Sign Aquarius*

Today you may feel a drive to renew things. Perhaps you are thinking about trading in your car, or considering new furniture for your house. Whatever it might be, shop around in order to make sure you get the best bargain possible. In some respects you could find yourself entering a slightly lazy streak.

25 SATURDAY   *Moon Age Day 21   Moon Sign Aquarius*

This would be a great time to plan a trip out, even if it is only to somewhere fairly local. You are quite likely to become bored with routine at the moment and would respond very positively to a complete change. A few hours away would make all the difference because you will return ready to get going.

26 SUNDAY   *Moon Age Day 22   Moon Sign Aquarius*

With everything to play for and things generally seeming to go your way, you can afford to take a few chances now. Your assessment of the way others are likely to behave will be second to none and you have what it takes to give a great deal to life and to reap a few major rewards as a result.

27 MONDAY   *Moon Age Day 23   Moon Sign Pisces*

There could be encounters with important new friends today, even if you don't realise that this is what is happening. People you only know casually at the moment could easily become significant in your life as time goes by. You are extremely articulate at present and should have no problem explaining yourself to anyone.

28 TUESDAY   *Moon Age Day 24   Moon Sign Pisces*

You need to see both sides of any coin today before you make up your mind one way or another. This is as true with regard to any professional offer that comes along as it is to friends who are having a disagreement. In the latter instance you can be a good intermediary, but you need to listen carefully first.

29 WEDNESDAY   *Moon Age Day 25   Moon Sign Aries*

Seek out new social contacts wherever you can find them and stay as close to the centre of what is happening in your own world as you can. There isn't really much time to retreat into yourself at present, not if you want to grasp hold of every fleeting possibility for gain and general advancement.

30 THURSDAY
Moon Age Day 26   Moon Sign Aries

If you are at work today you should discover that a combination of determination and concentration could be formidable allies. That's just as well because some of the decisions you make at the moment can have a big part to play in the way situations work out much further down the road.

31 FRIDAY
Moon Age Day 27   Moon Sign Aries

A friend might have some valuable information for you today and it comes along at what is almost certainly the most opportune time. Remain on your guard for some duplicity, though this is certainly not likely to come from the direction of people you know well and care for. Work related matters should run fairly smoothly.

2019

1 SATURDAY
Moon Age Day 28   Moon Sign Taurus

Use the energy that is around at present to get on with something you see as very important. This might be difficult in a professional sense but the weekend could offer you the chance to clear the decks for action early next week. There should also be enough time to make fun for others and to enjoy it yourself.

2 SUNDAY
Moon Age Day 29   Moon Sign Taurus

Perhaps this isn't the most stable day of the month as far as your personal life is concerned but much depends on the way you approach situations. Don't get uptight about little things and allow others to have the benefit of the doubt. The Crab is probably a little tense at the moment.

3 MONDAY
Moon Age Day 0   Moon Sign Gemini

Along comes a day that is perfect for expansive thinking. There are no limits to your imagination at present so all those outrageous plans for the future can blossom and grow in your dreams. Encourage others to join you on your flights of fantasy because that is where reality is born.

4 TUESDAY
Moon Age Day 1   Moon Sign Gemini

This is a time during which insight and awareness prove to be extremely important. Have a clear out of anything that might be holding you back and don't hang on to outmoded ways of thinking. Others might play games now but what you say goes right to the heart of most matters.

5 WEDNESDAY
Moon Age Day 2   Moon Sign Cancer

Worrying about your own limitations isn't something you are likely to be doing at all today. On the contrary you might believe you are capable of almost anything. Cancer is now braver than usual and that means you could take some calculated risks. Better to stick to the difficult rather than to try for the impossible, however.

6 THURSDAY
Moon Age Day 3   Moon Sign Cancer

You might enjoy a little good luck under today's planetary trends. The number of gains that come your way is directly proportional to your strength of character and your ability to adapt yourself in any situation. Since you have an abundance of energy, it is possible to get through lots of jobs, even before lunch.

7 FRIDAY
Moon Age Day 4   Moon Sign Leo

You now have it within your power to bring out the very best in others. This is not just the case in the practical world but extends into your personal life too. As a result the day should be quite pleasant. Don't allow shadows from the past to have a bearing on your present life and circumstances.

8 SATURDAY
Moon Age Day 5   Moon Sign Leo

Good financial planning and sensible budgeting will ensure that you get through the coming week with your bank balance intact. Don't be tempted by bargains because they could turn out to be anything but what they seem. There is just a chance you might fall prey to some sort of confidence trick.

9 SUNDAY
Moon Age Day 6   Moon Sign Virgo

This should be an enjoyable Sunday, when you enjoy a good exchange of ideas and opinions with others. At the same time you will need some change and diversity and so might not be inclined to spend too much time at home. Get out and about, preferably in the company of people you like a great deal.

10 MONDAY
Moon Age Day 7   Moon Sign Virgo

Although this remains a time of high energy, it is not necessarily the case that this will be translated into personal progress. Although you should find concentration comes easily, you may have a tendency to scatter your efforts among too many projects. Try not to tackle too many jobs at once.

11 TUESDAY
Moon Age Day 8   Moon Sign Virgo

As far as trying to broaden your horizons is concerned, this now looks like a good period. Someone seems to be making life rather interesting for you at present and you are inclined to enjoy yourself. Bending the truth might be something of a necessity if you don't want to give offence.

12 WEDNESDAY
Moon Age Day 9   Moon Sign Libra

Don't rush ahead with practical decisions at this time but wait until the time is right. How will you know? Simply use a combination of intuition and common sense and you won't go far wrong. Tedious tasks can be shared with people who seem only too willing to lend you a hand.

13 THURSDAY
Moon Age Day 10   Moon Sign Libra

Avoid arguments, particularly at home. These won't get you very far and might create difficulties that will be awkward to solve later. It is far better right now to walk away from a confrontational situation, even if your instincts are telling you that this might not be the right way forward.

14 FRIDAY
Moon Age Day 11   Moon Sign Scorpio

Some less than favourable trends now evaporate and this leaves you feeling more confident and happy to enjoy what life has to offer. People prove to be generally friendly and you are naturally more trusting than has been the case for some days. There are possible gains from small, measured speculations.

15 SATURDAY   *Moon Age Day 12   Moon Sign Scorpio*

You may be on the receiving end of some useful information today and your thought process is clear enough for you to make the best of whatever you hear. Friends and family members alike should prove to be quite accommodating and there isn't much doubt about either your sincerity or your kindness.

16 SUNDAY   *Moon Age Day 13   Moon Sign Sagittarius*

Although you are still not exactly moving mountains in your desire to get ahead, there is a certain quiet dignity about you at the moment that others could hardly fail to recognise. With plenty of enthusiasm for new projects and an ability to look ahead, this ought to be a more useful day than you might initially think.

17 MONDAY   *Moon Age Day 14   Moon Sign Sagittarius*

There are some very interesting conversations taking place in your immediate vicinity and they offer you the chance to get ahead in ways you hadn't thought of before. With popularity definitely on your side this ought to be a positive interlude for making a good impression and getting what you want as a result.

18 TUESDAY   *Moon Age Day 15   Moon Sign Capricorn*

You might be more pessimistic than is good for you right now, and if this is the case you can blame the fact that the Moon is in your opposite zodiac sign. Your own practical skills seem to take a holiday and you might have to rely instead on the good offices of colleagues and friends. The important thing is to smile at your shortcomings.

19 WEDNESDAY   *Moon Age Day 16   Moon Sign Capricorn*

This is not the most auspicious day of the month. The lunar low is still around, so you can't expect miracles, especially from plans that have only just been laid. All that's wrong now is that you are impatient for results. Within a single day your whole attitude is likely to change so just wait a while.

20 THURSDAY   *Moon Age Day 17   Moon Sign Capricorn*

Although you could get off to a rather slow start today, this is no yardstick as to the distance you manage to run in some very important races. Active and enthusiastic, you are also extremely romantic at the moment. Enlist the support of someone who is a specialist in their own field and a person who has much to teach you.

21 FRIDAY   *Moon Age Day 18   Moon Sign Aquarius*

You seem to be in very high spirits today and can move the goalposts over issues that have been something of a stumbling block of late. Money matters should look better as a result and you can probably afford to spoil yourself a little. Take on some new hobby or pastime that really suits your mood.

22 SATURDAY   *Moon Age Day 19   Moon Sign Aquarius*

You seem to have a lot of energy at the moment and much of it is thrown into professional matters. There are certain problems around that only you can solve, which is why others are so willing to come to you today. Try to get a change of scenery at this stage of the weekend if at all possible.

23 SUNDAY   *Moon Age Day 20   Moon Sign Pisces*

When it comes to getting your own way this might prove to be one of the very best days in the whole of June. Of course, you have to ask yourself whether you really are all that interested in some of the projects you are taking on. Trends suggest that you will find time to show great consideration to those around you who have problems.

24 MONDAY   *Moon Age Day 21   Moon Sign Pisces*

There are new gains to be made at the start of this working week, mainly because you make sure you are where the action is. Active and enterprising, you can do a few good deals, even before the middle of the day. This ought to leave time later to get to grips with an interesting but quite demanding romantic phase.

25 TUESDAY
Moon Age Day 22   Moon Sign Pisces

Standard responses probably won't work now and you are likely to spend quite a lot of time today getting on side with others, some of whom prove to be quite awkward. Attitude is all-important but don't forget that not everything that goes slightly wrong is your fault. Simply be yourself and wait for a better day.

26 WEDNESDAY
Moon Age Day 23   Moon Sign Aries

Emotional security is on your mind and you could spend quite a lot of today making sure that everyone else around you is happy. When you come across someone who seems determined to be awkward there is probably nothing you can do except to monitor the situation and wait for a while.

27 THURSDAY
Moon Age Day 24   Moon Sign Aries

There are possible new alliances in professional matters and perhaps even a success that comes like a bolt from the blue. Getting to grips with the needs of your partner might not be all that easy but if you talk things through carefully and with patience you can bring almost anyone to your point of view.

28 FRIDAY
Moon Age Day 25   Moon Sign Taurus

This should be a good time for getting others to do your bidding, and without having to try very hard. Your intuition is especially strong at the moment and you have an instinct for what looks and feels right. If you have to appear in public today it will be important to make a good impression.

29 SATURDAY
Moon Age Day 26   Moon Sign Taurus

Today turns out better for Cancerians who don't work at the weekend. If you have to put in a shift today, let matters ride rather than falling out with colleagues. Socially speaking you ought to be on top form because in this area of your life there doesn't seem to be anything particularly important to prove.

30 SUNDAY   *Moon Age Day 27   Moon Sign Gemini*

Your imagination is working well and this is the first base towards making changes at home that really please you. Take on board the ideas and opinions of family members and incorporate these into any scheme that naturally occurs to you. Stretching yourself socially should not be at all hard today.

July 2019

1 MONDAY
Moon Age Day 28   Moon Sign Gemini

This is the best time of this week for taking the initiative. Don't let those around you make decisions that you know are yours by right and be willing to go that extra step to get what you want. The often-quiet Cancer can be the most determined and bloody-minded of the zodiac signs when it wants to be. Sometimes that's important.

2 TUESDAY
Moon Age Day 0   Moon Sign Gemini

Someone is likely to oppose you at this time, a situation that is almost certain to lead to frustration on your part. Acting on impulse is still important, though you might want to check one or two facts along the way. Romance is on the cards for some Cancerians and your general popularity is assured.

3 WEDNESDAY
Moon Age Day 1   Moon Sign Cancer

You now find yourself in a period during which you will be more willing to take risks than usual, and a time that simply resounds with possible successes, most of which come along as a result of your own efforts. Even though some of your ideas are unusual it should be possible for you to reach a receptive audience.

4 THURSDAY
Moon Age Day 2   Moon Sign Cancer

Fortune is now something you make for yourself but you won't say no to the odd helping hand. These may come partly through your present persuasive nature and also from your electric personality. You can certainly gain admirers now and might even find yourself fighting one or two of them off.

5 FRIDAY
Moon Age Day 3   Moon Sign Leo

This might prove to be a day on which you would rather do anything than cause a fuss. That could be a shame because if people are behaving in an unreasonable manner, they need to be told. Family members should not only prove supportive but will actively encourage your sometimes strange ideas.

6 SATURDAY
Moon Age Day 4   Moon Sign Leo

A fast pace of events in the social world could leave you quite dizzy but still enjoying what life has to offer. Don't be too quick to jump to conclusions, especially in relationships. If you do, and allow your jealousy to show, you might end up regretting your words and having to apologise.

7 SUNDAY
Moon Age Day 5   Moon Sign Virgo

Look out for a period of increased social activity and a time during which romantic overtures are far more likely. You have plenty of enthusiasm for new projects and an overwhelming desire to succeed for its own sake. You should feel especially confident when you know what is expected of you.

8 MONDAY
☿   *Moon Age Day 6   Moon Sign Virgo*

Someone older than you or in a position of authority may prove to be a strong motivating force in your life at present. This should be a very good day for work-related endeavours and also for showing what sporting acumen you have. Don't be too quick to criticise a friend or colleague.

9 TUESDAY
☿   *Moon Age Day 7   Moon Sign Libra*

You should now be doing as much as you can to increase your list of contacts. The more friends you have at the moment, the better. There are gains to be made as a result of looking ahead in the way that Cancer does well. You could also benefit simply from listening to what is being said around you.

10 WEDNESDAY ☿   *Moon Age Day 8*   *Moon Sign Libra*

Look out for a period of great intellectual inspiration and excitement. As far as meetings with others are generally concerned, this period can do you a great deal of good and lead to some pleasing agreements. Some will have difficulty in keeping up with your razor-sharp wit, so be prepared to have to explain yourself.

11 THURSDAY ☿   *Moon Age Day 9*   *Moon Sign Scorpio*

You might have to go over a recent project again quite carefully and this is a time when things need looking at with a good deal of scrutiny. It isn't that you are making mistakes, more that you insist on having everything just right. This could be something of a tall order.

12 FRIDAY ☿   *Moon Age Day 10*   *Moon Sign Scorpio*

Today is likely to bring romantic trends. You will doubtless feel like getting away from routines of any sort and all you really want to do today is to chat and be sociable. It doesn't really matter who you are mixing with either. What counts is that you are in amongst a throng – which isn't you as a rule.

13 SATURDAY ☿ *Moon Age Day 11*   *Moon Sign Sagittarius*

Maybe you are not getting enough exercise at present and if this is the case you are likely to be rather sluggish. What you need is fresh air and a different environment generally. That might be hard to arrange if you are busy at present but with a little manoeuvring you should manage the switch.

14 SUNDAY ☿ *Moon Age Day 12*   *Moon Sign Sagittarius*

Your interests tend to turn towards cultural matters around now. You have a very sensitive quality that makes others sit up and take notice. Anything old, unusual or downright odd is likely to attract your attention today and you turn up your intuition beam to super high.

15 MONDAY ☿ *Moon Age Day 13   Moon Sign Capricorn*

The lunar low might take the edge off today and brings a generally sluggish phase that lasts a day or two. To counteract these trends, get as many changes into your life as you can and don't allow yourself to be forced down paths that are not of your own choosing. Friends could prove to be very supportive.

16 TUESDAY ☿ *Moon Age Day 14   Moon Sign Capricorn*

Your general spirits and your capacity for success might be slightly diminished but bear in mind that this is a very temporary thing. Some Cancerians will negate the lunar low altogether by simply turning their attention in different directions. With just a little thought, you could be one of them.

17 WEDNESDAY ☿ *Moon Age Day 15   Moon Sign Capricorn*

To a great extent you create your own opportunities between now and the weekend and it should not be difficult to get people to take notice of you. Although you might feel as though someone in your vicinity has little or no time for you, it is possible that for once you are completely wrong.

18 THURSDAY ☿ *Moon Age Day 16   Moon Sign Aquarius*

Look out for special times that come like a bolt from the blue. Although the main thrust of life might seem somewhat slow, others can enliven your day no end, simply by saying and doing the right things. What could be real pessimism at the beginning of the day might soon change as the hours advance.

19 FRIDAY ☿ *Moon Age Day 17   Moon Sign Aquarius*

It isn't all that easy to stand up for yourself today or maybe it just doesn't seem all that important to do so. You have what it takes to please your partner and family members and it is towards these people that your mind continually turns. Present planetary trends could make you contemplative and probably quiet.

20 SATURDAY ☿ *Moon Age Day 18 Moon Sign Pisces*

Convince your partner, or family members, that you know what is best for them. If someone close to you really isn't thinking things through it may be up to you to redress the balance. A continued reliance on your intuition is understandable at the moment because it is unlikely to let you down.

21 SUNDAY ☿ *Moon Age Day 19 Moon Sign Pisces*

This is a day during which you would relish being out and about. Although not everyone seems to be in the same good mood as you, you have what is required to cheer up the whole world if you really want to. However, in one or two specific cases some aspects in your chart indicate that you might not be inclined to do so.

22 MONDAY ☿ *Moon Age Day 20 Moon Sign Pisces*

Someone you meet today, probably in a professional situation, has the power to inspire you to move on to bigger and better things. This is a day for paying attention in all areas of your life, however, because much is going your way. Sticking to everyday routines probably won't get you what you want and a little originality may be called for.

23 TUESDAY ☿ *Moon Age Day 21 Moon Sign Aries*

Colleagues ought to be especially helpful and considerate at this time but this is no more than you deserve because you have been showing such kindness yourself. It should not be hard to think of something to do at the moment; on the contrary, it's difficult to keep up with all the possibilities on offer.

24 WEDNESDAY ☿ *Moon Age Day 22 Moon Sign Aries*

A few little niggles are likely to get in the way of your contentment today and you will need to be prepared to change your mind, even when you are in the middle of something. While you have the confidence to do this, the help and support you had been expecting from others may not be quite as forthcoming as you had hoped.

25 THURSDAY ☿ *Moon Age Day 23 Moon Sign Taurus*

All in all this is likely to be a much quieter period than some you have experienced across the last few days. With time to sit and contemplate, as well as hours spent with your partner or family members, you will be luxuriating in a little relaxation. Make sure travel details for the future are dealt with today.

26 FRIDAY ☿ *Moon Age Day 24 Moon Sign Taurus*

Avoid tensions with loved ones by listening to what they are saying and also by offering your own advice as diplomatically as you can. Cancer is rarely harsh or blunt which is good as being so wouldn't help at the moment. Watch out for some small financial gains coming along at any time now.

27 SATURDAY ☿ *Moon Age Day 25 Moon Sign Taurus*

There are new planetary influences coming along now that should perk up the social scene no end. Not only are there people around who actively encourage you to make more of yourself but also you are now naturally inclined to chase positive situations. If you are embarking on a new educational process, so much the better.

28 SUNDAY ☿ *Moon Age Day 26 Moon Sign Gemini*

Your imagination is stimulated by almost everything you see and do today. The world will probably have more colour and the depth of your vision knows no bounds. One implication of this is that you see the way forward in a very different way to someone close to you and will have to find ways to explain your thinking.

29 MONDAY ☿ *Moon Age Day 27 Moon Sign Gemini*

You won't get everything you want today but you will probably have more than you need. Watch out for people who have authority and standing because these are the types who can be of most use to you at the moment. Your confidence grows slowly but surely regarding a major alteration at work for some Cancerians.

30 TUESDAY ☿ *Moon Age Day 28   Moon Sign Cancer*

Your progress should run smoothly today and the Moon entering your zodiac sign offers an opening to new possibilities in more than one sphere of your life. You need to be in the fast lane right now and won't have all that much sympathy with those who find it difficult to keep up.

31 WEDNESDAY ☿ *Moon Age Day 0   Moon Sign Cancer*

Trends suggest that a new project could come along and that it is one that will take all the resources you have if you are going to make the best of it. This period should also be good in a romantic sense and it will now be easier to find exactly the words you need to enliven your personal life more than at any time in the recent past.

August

2019

1 THURSDAY
Moon Age Day 1   Moon Sign Leo

This is a favourable time to expand your horizons but be sure that the advice others give you, though well intentioned, won't hold you back. You might have to refuse a favour and if this turns out to be the case make sure that you are tactful about how you do it.

2 FRIDAY
Moon Age Day 2   Moon Sign Leo

Right now you should be planning ahead in order to make something important possible. Although it might take you some time to work out what this might be, the effort is certainly worthwhile. Be bold and determined and listen to the very sensible advice of people who are older or more experienced than you are.

3 SATURDAY
Moon Age Day 3   Moon Sign Virgo

Some of your feelings could be rather too close to the surface at present, which means you will have to stifle them, at least for a day or two. Although this is not a useful strategy as a rule, it might be so now. The problem is that you are not looking at situations as dispassionately as you sometimes can.

4 SUNDAY
Moon Age Day 4   Moon Sign Virgo

Group based relationships prove to be very rewarding, as does co-operation of almost any sort. Although not everyone agrees with your point of view at the moment, when it matters the most you won't have too much trouble bringing people round to your opinion. Affairs of the heart flourish.

5 MONDAY
Moon Age Day 5   Moon Sign Libra

The need to assert yourself and to debate issues is quite strong at the start of this week. Don't allow this to turn into an argumentative phase because this won't do you any good at all. In a romantic sense it is likely that you are on the receiving end of compliments you simply didn't expect.

6 TUESDAY
Moon Age Day 6   Moon Sign Libra

Although you won't be exactly speeding towards your objectives today you will move forward slowly and steadily. Arrangements for meetings or journeys may have to be altered at the last minute and you could experience a little personal frustration if your partner has different ideas from yours.

7 WEDNESDAY
Moon Age Day 7   Moon Sign Scorpio

You might not be especially inclined to push yourself too hard and may enjoy a little luxury in your life instead. The attitude of friends may be a little odd, that is until you ask a few leading questions. This would be a great time to be thinking in terms of some new hobby or pastime.

8 THURSDAY
Moon Age Day 8   Moon Sign Scorpio

Your chart reveals tremendous scope for relaxation today and for spending a few hours enjoying yourself. For the Crab this might be as simple as a long rest in a comfortable hammock – or it could be climbing a mountain. Whatever your personal ambition might be, this is the time to go for it.

9 FRIDAY
Moon Age Day 9   Moon Sign Sagittarius

Good news is likely to arrive around now and it might come from a long way off. However, you must remain cautious as this is no time for the Crab to count its chickens before they have hatched. What you do have on your side at the moment is great cheerfulness and a fairly high opinion of your own capabilities.

10 SATURDAY *Moon Age Day 10 Moon Sign Sagittarius*

There should be much about family life that will keep you reassured and happy with your lot. This would be an excellent time to travel and if you have planned your holidays around now, so much the better. Rules and regulations are likely to get on your nerves, unless you are the one making them.

11 SUNDAY *Moon Age Day 11 Moon Sign Sagittarius*

People like you because you try so hard and it is likely that they will back you, even when things go slightly awry. There are gains to be made from very limited speculations but in the main you should keep your money in your purse or pocket today. The most important Sunday events don't cost much at present.

12 MONDAY *Moon Age Day 12 Moon Sign Capricorn*

There is likely to be some inactivity today, especially in a professional sense. The arrival of the lunar low for August may well be the signal for you to be taking it easy. Look for places with wide-open vistas or falling water. The Crab deserves a break now so make the most of the August weather.

13 TUESDAY *Moon Age Day 13 Moon Sign Capricorn*

This is another day on which getting things done in a practical sense isn't going to be all that easy, so you may as well relax. If you insist on starting new projects you will probably only have to begin again later so you may as well spend your time planning instead. Do it somewhere really pleasant.

14 WEDNESDAY *Moon Age Day 14 Moon Sign Aquarius*

In a social sense, your hopes tend to be fired up now. There are some interesting people about and you may find yourself making contact with someone who is going to prove especially important and fortunate in your life. Your confidence grows regarding a plan that has taken up a good deal of your time already.

15 THURSDAY   *Moon Age Day 15   Moon Sign Aquarius*

If you are searching for new attachments of almost any sort you could do worse than to look around right now. People generally seem to be interested in you and are only too willing to put themselves out on your behalf. Romantic attachments should be starting to look slightly more exciting today.

16 FRIDAY   *Moon Age Day 16   Moon Sign Aquarius*

You should enjoy being on the move today and will be starting as you mean to go on, particularly at work. You show great determination when faced with obstacles that would once have held you back. In matters of health, your chart indicates that you should keep away from substances you know you have reacted against in the past and try for a healthy life.

17 SATURDAY   *Moon Age Day 17   Moon Sign Pisces*

You may need to keep personal plans and ambitions to a minimum at the moment. The fact is that some of the planetary helpers that have been around you of late are not quite so obliging today. Don't get bogged down with red tape but do your best to keep plodding along steadily, at least for now.

18 SUNDAY   *Moon Age Day 18   Moon Sign Pisces*

Communication is the way out of any jam. You are good when put on the spot now and can be more or less guaranteed to come up with the right remark. Although you are still only moving forward very slowly, you should be able to see your way ahead slightly more clearly. Your partner should be especially responsive.

19 MONDAY   *Moon Age Day 19   Moon Sign Aries*

Your mind seems to dwell on the past more than would usually be the case. This is fine if you are looking for answers to present conundrums but isn't much help if you are simply being nostalgic for its own sake. A good commitment to an idea put forward by a colleague could be the way forward.

20 TUESDAY
Moon Age Day 20   Moon Sign Aries

When it comes to the private side of your life you might have a few doubts and might want to confide in someone you trust. Not everyone is behaving in quite the way you might have come to expect and this could include your partner. Stand by a decision you have made at home, but not too forcefully.

21 WEDNESDAY
Moon Age Day 21   Moon Sign Aries

Don't allow yourself to become unrealistic regarding a romantic or personal matter. As the day advances you should discover that your drive and enthusiasm are increasing and that means putting in a little more effort. Most of your hopes and wishes at the moment relate specifically to domestic and family situations.

22 THURSDAY
Moon Age Day 22   Moon Sign Taurus

Relationships are likely to work out better at this time, supported by an astrological trend that also finds you seeking answers to old problems. This would be a great time for burying a hatchet and for letting go of something from the past that has no real part to play in your life from now on.

23 FRIDAY
Moon Age Day 23   Moon Sign Taurus

Your natural curiosity is definitely much heightened right now and you are examining things more closely than would usually be the case. Get away from tedious situations that bore you and don't be afraid to make up your mind at short notice. Your general popularity is high and new friends are a possibility.

24 SATURDAY
Moon Age Day 24   Moon Sign Gemini

On a material level you will probably have most of what you need for now, though you might be urged by others to cast your mind ahead and to plan for the distant future. This would not be a particularly good time to sign documents or to make decisions that will be with you for years and years.

25 SUNDAY
Moon Age Day 25   Moon Sign Gemini

There ought to be plenty about today that seems very rewarding. The only slight drawback could come from the fact that certain other people are not fulfilling their obligations in the way you might wish. It could be that you are expecting rather too much of them in the first place so have a think.

26 MONDAY
Moon Age Day 26   Moon Sign Cancer

You will now be looking for ingenious ways to get ahead and can gain a great deal simply from showing how versatile you are. There are many people around at present who love your style and the way you achieve your objectives. Love is likely to come knocking at your door at any time this week.

27 TUESDAY
Moon Age Day 27   Moon Sign Cancer

Another good day is in store, not least of all because of your own very positive attitude. Even casual remarks made by others can set you off on a new adventure. Itemise your needs and wants in the almost certain knowledge that they will be fulfilled. The more positive you are, the better.

28 WEDNESDAY
Moon Age Day 28   Moon Sign Leo

This may be the best day for ages with regard to romance. Personally speaking it is likely that life has simply been jogging along of late but better astrological trends can bring significant joy. Something may happen to make you acutely aware of the need family members have of you at this time.

29 THURSDAY
Moon Age Day 29   Moon Sign Leo

In a material sense you are now in a position to do yourself a great deal of good. This probably comes from a mixture of careful planning and in-depth discussions. Although you may also find one or two irritants troubling you throughout today, you should be able to deal with them as and when they arise.

30 FRIDAY
Moon Age Day 0   Moon Sign Virgo

If there is something to celebrate at home, get stuck in and do some of the organising. You can really find joy in the success of others at this time and to do so also makes you forget some of your own cares. By the time you get back to them, at least a couple could have disappeared altogether.

31 SATURDAY
Moon Age Day 1   Moon Sign Virgo

Keep your eyes and ears open for new information that is coming your way at any time now. Personal projects are especially well highlighted and you have what it takes to change situations to your own advantage. Love looks good and especially for those Crabs who are in the market for a new romance.

September
2019

1 SUNDAY
Moon Age Day 2   Moon Sign Libra

It might seem easier to take shortcuts today but in the end it will only cause you more problems. By far the best way forward now is to do fewer jobs but to do them to the very best of your ability. Don't worry if you find you are out of your depth on some occasions because help is at hand.

2 MONDAY
Moon Age Day 3   Moon Sign Libra

You definitely have the desire to spread your wings and although this might not be possible during a normal working day, there does not appear to be anything to prevent you planning ahead. People you only know in a casual sense might have plenty to say to you now, some of which could be very interesting.

3 TUESDAY
Moon Age Day 4   Moon Sign Scorpio

Planetary trends suggest that Cancer is in a slightly disagreeable frame of mind today and could easily get on the wrong side of someone whose friendship it should be cultivating. It's fair enough that you don't want to allow yourself to be walked on, but deal with others as tactfully as you can.

4 WEDNESDAY
Moon Age Day 5   Moon Sign Scorpio

Trends move on and now you are willing to give and take with the best of them. This enhances your popularity and means that people in your environment take more notice of your presence. If you have been feeling slightly out of sorts recently, things should be looking better quite soon.

5 THURSDAY *Moon Age Day 6 Moon Sign Scorpio*

The time might be more than right to dump some of the excess baggage you have been carrying around for quite some time. This includes the problems of people who will do nothing to sort things out on their own account and who naturally assume that you will carry their load for them.

6 FRIDAY *Moon Age Day 7 Moon Sign Sagittarius*

Not everyone is going to turn out to be as loyal as you had hoped and this fact could lead to a few disappointments. All you can really do is to shrug your shoulders and move on. If you do feel yourself to be let down in some areas, you can be sure that support arrives in others and that friends will come good for you.

7 SATURDAY *Moon Age Day 8 Moon Sign Sagittarius*

You definitely need to be as assertive as possible in your dealings with the outside world now. Work matters ought to run smoothly enough but it is probably towards your social life that your mind turns time and again whilst you are otherwise engaged. Take heart from the fact that you are more adaptable than you think today.

8 SUNDAY *Moon Age Day 9 Moon Sign Capricorn*

The Crab is much in demand at present and that means you could be spreading yourself rather too thinly. Don't try to be all things to all people because it won't work. When you are natural, those around you find you excellent company. Opt for a change in domestic routines if you can today and offer strong support to family members.

9 MONDAY *Moon Age Day 10 Moon Sign Capricorn*

You feel the need to retreat from the cut and thrust of everyday life at this time, which is not so strange with the Moon in your opposite sign. As a result, you might be inclined to be quieter than of late and won't seem to have the same amount of time for others.

10 TUESDAY · · · · · · · · · *Moon Age Day 11 · · · Moon Sign Aquarius*

Along comes a brand new phase, during which you are happy to do things with others. During this time, the more you co-operate, the greater are the rewards on offer. It won't always be easy but the results make the effort worthwhile and you might well gain some new friends on the way.

11 WEDNESDAY · · · *Moon Age Day 12 · · · Moon Sign Aquarius*

The right opportunities are not far away now, and it is possible that much of your thoughts are taken up with the possibility of travel. Even short journeys can be of great interest and it isn't out of the question that some Cancerians will be embarking on the journey of a lifetime, either now or quite soon.

12 THURSDAY · · · · · · *Moon Age Day 13 · · · Moon Sign Aquarius*

Relatives and even friends might be only too willing to lend a timely hand and will also be quite ready with advice. In the end you have to decide things for yourself and that's something that comes easier today. Not everyone has your best interests at heart and your intuition will tell you who to trust.

13 FRIDAY · · · · · · · · · · *Moon Age Day 14 · · · Moon Sign Pisces*

A sense of urgency exists regarding emotional matters, though you would be best advised not to get into deep discussions for the next day or two. Keep life light and easy and you won't feel in any way restricted. The fact is that quite a few issues will look very different even by tomorrow.

14 SATURDAY · · · · · · · · · *Moon Age Day 15 · · · Moon Sign Pisces*

Getting on with a number of different jobs at the same time is really very easy for you at present. Almost from the moment you get out of bed you are likely to be active and enterprising. Dealing with routine tasks should be less of a problem than was the case yesterday. Your social inclinations are strong.

15 SUNDAY *Moon Age Day 16   Moon Sign Aries*

Every problem has a rational answer – this is true even for issues that have dogged you for quite some time. Once you have looked at matters carefully you will be able to deal with a number of issues. This is a Sunday during which you will want to make the best of any remaining good weather to get out into the fresh air.

16 MONDAY *Moon Age Day 17   Moon Sign Aries*

You should be able to keep up a varied and interesting schedule today, most of which comes about as a result of your own choices. Be ready to open yourself up to new situations, especially those of a social nature. At the same time you should notice that your influence on the world at large is on the rise.

17 TUESDAY *Moon Age Day 18   Moon Sign Aries*

You are sensitive to the needs of others at the moment and easily able to put yourself in their shoes. As a result you will be putting yourself out significantly on their behalf and can get a good deal of respect as a result. The really brave side of Cancer is likely to be on display for the next couple of days.

18 WEDNESDAY *Moon Age Day 19   Moon Sign Taurus*

Group activities would probably be a lot of fun now and you have what it takes to be at the centre of any organisation that is going on. Don't try to achieve everything all at once but be willing to wait a little. Your confidence to do the right thing remains generally strong and the midweek period should be fun.

19 THURSDAY *Moon Age Day 20   Moon Sign Taurus*

The chances are that you will be quite emotional today and this means you might be a little reluctant to take a chance where a particular relationship is concerned. Also, there are financial gains to be made, even if you don't seem to have that much control over what they are and how they turn out.

20 FRIDAY   *Moon Age Day 21   Moon Sign Gemini*

You may feel restless today, and if so getting out and about will be very important to you. When you have made up your mind to a particular course of action it is very unlikely that you would alter your opinion, though you do at least need to give the impression that you are open to persuasion.

21 SATURDAY   *Moon Age Day 22   Moon Sign Gemini*

It looks as though you now have the necessary motivation to seek out new friends and to try experiences that haven't been a part of your life until now. There might not be anything particularly comfortable about today but you will have plenty of enthusiasm and a desire to get where you want to go.

22 SUNDAY   *Moon Age Day 23   Moon Sign Gemini*

Although you are still generally on the ball, there are aspects of your thinking right now that others might see as slightly irrational. The odd thing is that no matter what direction you take to gain your objectives, everything is likely to work out well for you in the end. This is not a day for undue anxiety.

23 MONDAY   *Moon Age Day 24   Moon Sign Cancer*

The lunar high should help you significantly and offers you an increased level of confidence. Be prepared to stick your neck out in situations where you know your attitude to be sensible and your desires modest. Few people will deny you your moment of glory around now.

24 TUESDAY   *Moon Age Day 25   Moon Sign Cancer*

You are still firing on all cylinders and anxious to make the best of impressions. Today should be good for romance, with overtures perhaps coming from fairly surprising directions and someone making the running with a chat-up line. Finding just the right sort of people to give you a leg up won't be at all hard today.

25 WEDNESDAY   *Moon Age Day 26   Moon Sign Leo*

Don't stay at home today more than you have to. You need change and diversity and can find this almost anywhere, just as long as you vary your routines. If you find yourself in a strange town or city, take time to enjoy some of the cultural interests on offer. Too many rules won't impress you now.

26 THURSDAY   *Moon Age Day 27   Moon Sign Leo*

You might just have to put up with some inconvenience today. This is likely to come from the direction of others because certain people seem to have 'awkward' as their middle name! Although this might hold your own progress back a little, you will play the Good Samaritan all the same.

27 FRIDAY   *Moon Age Day 28   Moon Sign Virgo*

You may find it difficult to cope if you decide to take on too many tasks at the same time today, which is why pacing yourself would be a very good idea. Remember what your strengths are and concentrate on them. Don't forget the needs of someone you don't see too often but for whom you have the greatest regard.

28 SATURDAY   *Moon Age Day 0   Moon Sign Virgo*

A slight reversal of trends for the next couple of days allows you to tackle several different tasks at the same time. The Moon is strong in your chart making you very chatty this weekend. Although there may well be practical issues to address, don't forget that you also need some time out to paint the town red.

29 SUNDAY   *Moon Age Day 1   Moon Sign Libra*

The everyday running of life might be subject to bumps of one sort or another but you will take these in your stride and will even laugh at some of the slight hiccups that come along. This is not a good time to be brooding on the past and instead keep your eyes firmly on the future.

30 MONDAY

Moon Age Day 2   Moon Sign Libra

You have a strong desire to succeed and will be pushing hard towards specific objectives, even if the social possibilities surrounding you at the moment sometimes get in the way a little. It also looks as though you might not have quite the say you would wish when alterations come along at home.

October 2019

1 TUESDAY
Moon Age Day 3   Moon Sign Scorpio

Avoid any sort of deception at the moment. Don't allow yourself to be drawn into any situation involving even white lies, and opt instead to say nothing at all. Friends can be quite helpful, although unfortunately sorting out the problems they inadvertently cause may be quite time consuming.

2 WEDNESDAY
Moon Age Day 4   Moon Sign Scorpio

It looks as though there will be disruptions and difficulties to be dealt with today, together with a few resultant frustrations. It consequently won't be too surprising to discover that you are going to be somewhat held back in your plans, although a little ingenuity can help you get over the obstacles.

3 THURSDAY
Moon Age Day 5   Moon Sign Sagittarius

Enjoy what today has to offer and don't allow yourself to be restricted by people who don't have a great deal of influence over your life as a whole. Someone you haven't seen for quite some time might be making a return visit to your life around now. This could cause a wave of nostalgia to sweep over you.

4 FRIDAY
Moon Age Day 6   Moon Sign Sagittarius

Trends indicate that you have plenty of energy today, but it is possible that your partner or perhaps close personal friends are less dynamic. A little gentle persuasion on your part can now go a long way and might get people going when they would otherwise prefer to let you make the running. Be bold when it comes to asking for what you want.

5 SATURDAY   *Moon Age Day 7*   *Moon Sign Capricorn*

The Moon is now presently in your opposite zodiac sign, making you less than certain about your thoughts and actions. In a way that is a pity because when it comes to any sort of planning you are actually second to none right now. You might have to give way to others in family matters.

6 SUNDAY   *Moon Age Day 8*   *Moon Sign Capricorn*

Your confidence is not all it might be today but this is only likely to bother you if you insist on pushing forward against the odds. Do the absolute least for now and let others take the strain. In the meantime try to find some moments to simply sit and dream; this is important for the Crab now and again.

7 MONDAY   *Moon Age Day 9*   *Moon Sign Capricorn*

It is possible that you will have to reorganise certain aspects of your day and that won't please you. Take heart from the fact that in the end things may turn out better as a result of the alterations. A few unaccountable mishaps won't prevent the Crab from getting where it wants to be.

8 TUESDAY   *Moon Age Day 10*   *Moon Sign Aquarius*

It shouldn't be hard to find the right words to make someone else feel particularly good about themselves. As a result they will make a greater fuss of you and might even be willing to put in that extra bit of effort on your behalf. From a material point of view you could find this period quite useful.

9 WEDNESDAY   *Moon Age Day 11*   *Moon Sign Aquarius*

In terms of your personal life today, a few of the slight disappointments you might have encountered recently look likely to be reversed and a much-valued apology could be coming your way. All the same, everything is not going to be quite what it seems so use a little circumspection.

10 THURSDAY · · · · · · · · *Moon Age Day 12* · · *Moon Sign Pisces*

Fewer demands placed upon you today find you with more time to do exactly what you want, especially at the end of the working day. In at least one practical sense you should now be quite close to a treasured objective, though you will have to pay particular attention if you want to find out what this is likely to be.

11 FRIDAY · · · · · · · · · · · *Moon Age Day 13* · · *Moon Sign Pisces*

Try to recognise the fact that you may be holding on to past events that you should let go. Use at least part of today to catch up and to sort out problems that have been around for a while. Once they are dealt with, you should be satisfied and feel able to move forward more productively than for days.

12 SATURDAY · · · · · · · · · *Moon Age Day 14* · · *Moon Sign Pisces*

There are real gains to be made right now and the material considerations of life must be part of the scenario. The general level of energy you are currently feeling is only going to rise and that means keeping extremely busy and enjoying a generally favourable time. You will already have next week in your sights.

13 SUNDAY · · · · · · · · · · · *Moon Age Day 15* · · *Moon Sign Aries*

Today proves to be a time during which the sheer force of your personality dazzles the world in general. The feeling of power that you are experiencing is not common for you, although this is in reality the way you appear to others who don't know about your lack of self confidence.

14 MONDAY · · · · · · · · · · *Moon Age Day 16* · · *Moon Sign Aries*

Make sure you are looking and listening at the start of this week because there are situations that could work to your advantage. Routines should be easily dealt with, though not all that welcome in some instances. If you find you are suffering from a degree of wanderlust, by all means do something about it.

15 TUESDAY
Moon Age Day 17   Moon Sign Taurus

Monetary developments appear to be an area of growth worth looking at carefully at this stage of this week. From a social point of view, there are some interesting times to be had and you could find yourself mixing with some less than likely individuals. What you will yearn for is excitement.

16 WEDNESDAY
Moon Age Day 18   Moon Sign Taurus

Keep your eyes and ears open for news, views and even gossip. You won't want to miss anything today and have exactly what it takes to turn what you see and hear into gold. Don't be afraid to discuss your latest plans with people who are likely to be in a position to give you some invaluable assistance.

17 THURSDAY
Moon Age Day 19   Moon Sign Taurus

Beware of possible deception today, which could come from any direction. It might be that people who are themselves in the dark are misleading you and some investigation is clearly called for. Enjoyable periods could come from the strangest directions right now, but don't knock it!

18 FRIDAY
Moon Age Day 20   Moon Sign Gemini

Your general position could seem weaker today, but this is probably just a perception based on the fact that you are not looking at things as positively as you might. It is important to believe in yourself and not to allow little failures to become your focus. If things do go wrong, pick up the pieces and start again immediately.

19 SATURDAY
Moon Age Day 21   Moon Sign Gemini

Problems in your love life might seem more trouble than they are worth today, but you know in your own heart that this is not the case. If you feel as though you are taking something of a battering at the moment, turn to a good friend and laugh away your little troubles in their company. You will feel great as a result.

20 SUNDAY
Moon Age Day 22   Moon Sign Cancer

Without any doubt this is the best time of the month to chance your arm a little. Although you are right to be cautious with cash, be aware that trends are very good right now. Always think through any decisions before you act, though. The lunar high makes you actively seek out fun, not simply for yourself but on account of anyone who is important in your life.

21 MONDAY
Moon Age Day 23   Moon Sign Cancer

The positive trends continue and find you pretty much in the pink. Enjoying general popularity, it won't be hard for you to persuade your partner that plans you are thinking up for the future are progressive and sensible. Almost anyone is convinced by your considerable charm at the moment.

22 TUESDAY
Moon Age Day 24   Moon Sign Leo

You now enter a period during which you are likely to be taking the emotional side of life fairly seriously. You might be just a little too sensitive for your own good on occasions and you must keep in mind the high regard that others have for you. Not a good day for any kind of financial risk.

23 WEDNESDAY
Moon Age Day 25   Moon Sign Leo

The general pace of life may seem to be slowing a little but that doesn't really apply to the more social aspects that present themselves later in the day. Take full advantage of any chance to get out on the town, possibly with friends, and avoid spending all your spare time in front of the television.

24 THURSDAY
Moon Age Day 26   Moon Sign Virgo

Look out for a phase in your love life during which communication could be something of a problem. As long as you realise this and take the appropriate steps, all should be well. What you don't want to be accused of at the moment is playing all your cards too close to your chest.

25 FRIDAY
Moon Age Day 27   Moon Sign Virgo

You need to be where the action is, especially when it comes to the more practical side of life. If you don't get yourself involved others will be making decisions on your behalf and that is not something you would want. In everyday life you could be breaking rules, or at the very least bending them significantly.

26 SATURDAY
Moon Age Day 28   Moon Sign Libra

You can make a very big impact on someone at the moment and will be quite certain about your attitude to almost anything. Positive thinking finds you in a position to overturn difficulties that were evident a few days ago and you can persuade anyone to do just about anything if you set your mind to it.

27 SUNDAY
Moon Age Day 0   Moon Sign Libra

Planetary trends further favour communications now, making this a time during which you can see good in just about anything. You will need to be just a little circumspect before taking on more than you can reasonably manage. It isn't now that the chickens come home to roost but a week or more into the future.

28 MONDAY
Moon Age Day 1   Moon Sign Scorpio

You should be getting where you want to be in a general sense and should not have too many problems persuading the world that you know what you are talking about. Silver-tongued and enchanting, you may be more popular at this stage of the month than has been the case for weeks.

29 TUESDAY
Moon Age Day 2   Moon Sign Scorpio

Daily matters not only keep you happily on the go but also contain much interesting information. Virtually nothing passes you by right now and you can make a silk purse out of a sow's ear in quite a number of ways. You might have a secret admirer, which although gratifying in one way could be embarrassing in another.

30 WEDNESDAY   *Moon Age Day 3   Moon Sign Sagittarius*

Though ambitions remain strong at the moment you really need to look at life's finer details. Attitude is very important when approaching others, especially so if you want to get them on your side. You can progress quite well but the fact that others are awkward could get in the way slightly.

31 THURSDAY   *Moon Age Day 4   Moon Sign Sagittarius*

This is one of the best times during the entire month to engage in social activities, so perhaps organise a Halloween party! The more the merrier seems to be your present adage and you even manage to smile upon those you haven't cared for that much in the past. You are quite flexible in your attitude at present, which certain of your friends will find a relief.

November
2019

1 FRIDAY
☿ *Moon Age Day 5 Moon Sign Sagittarius*

Avoid being too bossy with friends, especially ones who clearly have your best interests at heart. Don't listen too much to gossip because it probably won't get you very far and stick to what you know to be the truth of any situation, no matter what others say to the contrary.

2 SATURDAY
☿ *Moon Age Day 6 Moon Sign Capricorn*

Perhaps you shouldn't over-estimate yourself and your capacities at the moment. The lunar low is likely to hold you back somewhat at the start of the weekend and could promote some doubts that already exist in your mind. Just give yourself a day or two to relax a little and then come back fighting.

3 SUNDAY
☿ *Moon Age Day 7 Moon Sign Capricorn*

If you are feeling a certain amount of anxiety related to matters that are completely beyond your control, stop to think about if there is anything you can do to change circumstances. If the answer is no, what is the point of worrying about them? Keep faith with life through its present twists and happier times will lie ahead.

4 MONDAY
☿ *Moon Age Day 8 Moon Sign Aquarius*

Try to create as many light-hearted moments as you can at the start of this working week. Some sort of stress is likely to be lifted from you now, leaving you feeling that you can move forward progressively. It is important to ignore things that are being said by people who clearly know nothing.

5 TUESDAY ☿ *Moon Age Day 9 Moon Sign Aquarius*

Getting what you want from life shouldn't be difficult now if you use a combination of your natural charm and a good deal of confidence. There may be changes to be made in specific areas of your life and now is as good a time as any to put some of them in place. You need to have strong plans laid by the end of the year.

6 WEDNESDAY ☿ *Moon Age Day 10 Moon Sign Pisces*

The things you hear from others this Wednesday might turn out to be quite useful and can be the base of new actions you find yourself anxious to take. There could be a few frustrations, possibly coming from the direction of loved ones, some of whom won't approve of either your attitude or some of your present friends.

7 THURSDAY ☿ *Moon Age Day 11 Moon Sign Pisces*

Although there can be some slight misunderstandings in personal relationships, in a general sense you are getting on well with those around you. Someone might have a very special idea for Christmas that you will be happy to endorse. Your confidence is growing, even if it is taking some time.

8 FRIDAY ☿ *Moon Age Day 12 Moon Sign Pisces*

This can be quite an explosive interlude in terms of some relationships, though generally speaking not those that are closest to your heart. You are showing that you won't stand any nonsense and you certainly won't take much persuading to get involved in a heated family debate.

9 SATURDAY ☿ *Moon Age Day 13 Moon Sign Aries*

Your present popularity is based at least in part on your sensitivity. You seem to know exactly what makes those around you tick and when to show sympathy. It's true that you are not everyone's cup of tea but that would be virtually impossible. Do give yourself some credit for your successes today.

10 SUNDAY ☿ *Moon Age Day 14 Moon Sign Aries*

You can look forward to an expanded circle of friends at this time, with a special emphasis on people who are deliberately seeking you out for one reason or another. Being in the right place at the right time could easily lead to one or two small financial gains, whilst your general popularity remains solid.

11 MONDAY ☿ *Moon Age Day 15 Moon Sign Taurus*

This could be a day of highly charged emotions for some Cancerians. What spurs this off probably isn't remotely important – it's how you react that matters. The more you talk to people, the less likely you are to bottle things up. Younger family members may prove especially supportive.

12 TUESDAY ☿ *Moon Age Day 16 Moon Sign Taurus*

If you need to get a message across to someone you know well, this is the time to go for it. You have tremendous energy and could prove to be quite competitive today. Romance can blossom under present trends, especially if you have been looking towards the possibility of a new love.

13 WEDNESDAY ☿ *Moon Age Day 17 Moon Sign Taurus*

Benefits come from travel, change, alternative interests and using the strength of your own personality. You appear to be very confident, even on those occasions when nothing could be further from the truth. The Crab shows a distinct fascination for anything curious around this time.

14 THURSDAY ☿ *Moon Age Day 18 Moon Sign Gemini*

This could be a particularly good day when it comes to career matters and also affairs of the heart. It should be easy to tell others the way you feel, not least of all because you are in a very truthful frame of mind. People you probably haven't seen for ages return to your life quite soon.

15 FRIDAY ☿ *Moon Age Day 19 Moon Sign Gemini*

This is not a time during which you will be all that interested in diplomatic niceties. If you believe that someone is trying to dupe you or a person you care about, the chances are that you will insist on having your say. Just make sure you have your facts right before you begin to shoot from the hip.

16 SATURDAY ☿ *Moon Age Day 20 Moon Sign Cancer*

It isn't simply a case of maximising your own potential during the lunar high but also the benefits that come from the way others can guide you that leads to significant success. Don't be afraid to seek out a little help when you need it. Favours are being returned and with your popularity at the moment running so very high, nobody should refuse you.

17 SUNDAY ☿ *Moon Age Day 21 Moon Sign Cancer*

Personal decisions should be easy to make and are unlikely to be cluttered by either any sort of confusion or too much emotion. Your intellect and wit are razor sharp, so what can hold you back? People you have known for ages may contribute to a string of potential gains and successes that come along now.

18 MONDAY ☿ *Moon Age Day 22 Moon Sign Leo*

A rather self-assertive and quite a restless period comes along courtesy of the present position of the planet Mars. Don't lose your temper over issues that really are not worth the bother and use a little patience, especially when you are dealing with younger people.

19 TUESDAY ☿ *Moon Age Day 23 Moon Sign Leo*

You may be feeling pleasantly disposed to the world at large and even though you are busy you will find the time to make those around you happy. They in turn will take significant notice of you and listen very carefully to those Cancerian ideas. You instinctively know what looks and feels right now.

20 WEDNESDAY ☿ *Moon Age Day 24   Moon Sign Leo*

You need to concentrate today if you really want to get on but if you are not at work the picture will look significantly different. Social trends are also good and you continue to turn heads when it matters. An outing of some sort this evening might suit you down to the ground, especially with good friends along.

21 THURSDAY *Moon Age Day 25   Moon Sign Virgo*

You nearly always enjoy attending to the needs of others but never more so than seems to be the case right now. However, you need to take as well as give so don't get too embarrassed if someone wants to make a big fuss of you. Avoid jealousy where your partner or someone you are attracted to is concerned.

22 FRIDAY *Moon Age Day 26   Moon Sign Virgo*

If you are involved with group activities today you should be in your element. At the moment you are a very good team player, though don't be in the least surprised if the rest of the team look to you for advice. Routines are for the birds and you tend to make up most things as you go along.

23 SATURDAY *Moon Age Day 27   Moon Sign Libra*

Avoid confrontations that are brought about as a result of your ego, which is extremely well emphasised in your chart at the moment. You have what it takes to continue your present successful phase but will not do so if you insist on falling out with others over details. Let people have their say and then make up your mind.

24 SUNDAY *Moon Age Day 28   Moon Sign Libra*

You may get the chance to make money, but unfortunately you might also end up losing it. It's all a matter of balance and you can't afford to gamble under present trends. Although you are willing to stand up for yourself at this time it is possible that you will be going a little too far.

25 MONDAY *Moon Age Day 29   Moon Sign Scorpio*

Your thinking is sharp and your hunches are likely to be spot on in most situations. The only area of life in which you may have to exhibit a little care is domestically. It could be that your nearest and dearest don't have quite the regard for your opinions that they once had, or at least it seems that way.

26 TUESDAY *Moon Age Day 0   Moon Sign Scorpio*

Today could be rather less than satisfying at home, especially if you fail to take into account the opinions of those with whom you live. All in all, it might be better to spend some time away from home. Perhaps a pre-Christmas shopping spree would take your fancy or a journey to a place that interests you.

27 WEDNESDAY *Moon Age Day 1   Moon Sign Sagittarius*

You benefit from being demonstrative in an intimate relationship and you are showing a strongly extroverted attitude generally. Money matters are likely to be fairly strong, though you might have to put something by with Christmas now being so close. There are definite gains to be made in terms of simple friendship.

28 THURSDAY *Moon Age Day 2   Moon Sign Sagittarius*

You should see financial issues on a definite upswing. This is not only a time to build successfully on previous efforts but also a period during which you can afford to back your most recent hunches. Gains may come from some fairly unexpected places, like junk shops or market stalls for example.

29 FRIDAY *Moon Age Day 3   Moon Sign Capricorn*

Although things still run satisfactorily, you will notice a great slowing of pace today. The lunar low is the culprit and there is really nothing for it but to relax and ride it out for a couple of days. If you take today at face value and find pleasure where it naturally arises, you may not even notice the slower pace.

30 SATURDAY   *Moon Age Day 4   Moon Sign Capricorn*

Most objectives ought to be put on the back burner for the moment as you choose to relax a little. By tomorrow the lunar low will be out of the way but in the meantime let others take some of the strain. You will still be working hard but it might be difficult to make much in the way of progress.

December

2019

1 SUNDAY ☿ Moon Age Day 5 Moon Sign Virgo

Now you will be more anxious than ever to be out there in the world, working hard and making a real impression. There are some interesting people around at the moment and you will want to get to know as many of them as you possibly can. Someone you really like could be very complimentary towards you.

2 MONDAY ☿ Moon Age Day 6 Moon Sign Libra

You don't lack charisma and your confidence is growing by the minute. With a number of planetary influences working especially well for you, this is definitely the right time to tell people your innermost thoughts. Almost everyone will find your opinions and insights fascinating now.

3 TUESDAY ☿ Moon Age Day 7 Moon Sign Libra

This is a day during which it is more than possible to see well ahead of yourself. Arrangements of the social kind can enliven today no end and you appear to have all it takes to persuade others to look in your direction. You know how to turn heads and that could prove to be very useful both now and in the days to come.

4 WEDNESDAY ☿ Moon Age Day 8 Moon Sign Scorpio

Some compromise is clearly called for right now. This is especially true in personal relationships. Cancer can be very determined and even a little selfish on occasions and you would do well to realise that there is often more than one point of view. If you give ground now, the rewards later will be great.

5 THURSDAY ☿ *Moon Age Day 9   Moon Sign Scorpio*

It won't have escaped your attention that Christmas is just around the corner, though this might be the first time you have really stopped to think about arrangements. There are very good times in store but these will be enhanced if you put in that extra little bit of effort now to make sure everything is organised.

6 FRIDAY ☿ *Moon Age Day 10   Moon Sign Scorpio*

Any misunderstandings that come about today can be sorted out quickly enough, leaving you plenty of time to do whatever takes your fancy. The weekend is in view and you recognise the fact. The spirit of freedom and self-choice probably start today for many Cancerians. Don't be afraid to be in the spotlight.

7 SATURDAY *Moon Age Day 11   Moon Sign Sagittarius*

The level of your general success now is high, though this may show more in personal attachments than in practical matters. An open and forward-looking attitude is definitely called for at present and you won't go far wrong if you can be sure that you are speaking the truth as you genuinely see it.

8 SUNDAY *Moon Age Day 12   Moon Sign Sagittarius*

It isn't unusual for the Crab to be put upon by others. Even family members, whom you love so much, must be told if they are severely treading on your toes. If you make your point of view abundantly clear from the start, there won't be any misunderstandings later.

9 MONDAY *Moon Age Day 13   Moon Sign Capricorn*

Expect a very good start to the week and look forward to greater potential professionally and an easy-going situation in matters of the heart. Slowly but surely you are developing a far more optimistic frame of mind. This eventually permeates into every nook and cranny of your life. Don't worry, people will notice.

10 TUESDAY   *Moon Age Day 14   Moon Sign Capricorn*

Plans and objectives could be aided by being in possession of information. This comes from a number of different sources but you are made aware of it thanks to the intervention of others. Getting to grips with ideas that can't mature until well into the New Year could also make today interesting.

11 WEDNESDAY   *Moon Age Day 15   Moon Sign Aquarius*

There seems to be a great deal of ego and assertiveness around at the moment and at least some of it could be coming from your direction. You may be looking towards a period of very hard work in the near future and it won't help if you cause problems with the people who can best help you. A little humility now goes a long way.

12 THURSDAY   *Moon Age Day 16   Moon Sign Aquarius*

Under current trends you might have to be slightly more frugal than you would like. Perhaps you haven't got everything you need for Christmas yet, whilst at the same time money is short? With a little careful planning you can do what is necessary in terms of gifts whilst spending little and also having fun.

13 FRIDAY   *Moon Age Day 17   Moon Sign Aquarius*

A greater sense of self confidence comes along with today, which you can put down almost exclusively to the arrival of the lunar high. Most things are almost certain to go your way and you are tremendously determined. Your social life looks likely to be exceptionally busy both today and tomorrow.

14 SATURDAY   *Moon Age Day 18   Moon Sign Pisces*

It's possible you will be feeling lucky today. Games of chance are much more likely and your hunches are generally likely to pay off. Confidence isn't a problem but there could be just a tiny amount of frustration if the concentration on Christmas prevents you from making the progress you would wish.

15 SUNDAY — *Moon Age Day 19   Moon Sign Pisces*

You may crave physical comforts right now and be enlisting the support of loved ones in order to make sure you get them. Luxury appeals and you won't want to be putting yourself out any more than is strictly necessary. Because you are so lovable it is likely that you receive all the attention you desire.

16 MONDAY — *Moon Age Day 20   Moon Sign Pisces*

You are very generous at the moment and that's a good thing, not least of all because you tend to get back much more than you give in one way or another. This would be a good time to enter competitions and to test your skill against others. Social trends are particularly interesting and remain so for some time.

17 TUESDAY — *Moon Age Day 21   Moon Sign Aries*

With the accent now firmly on enjoyable communication with others, you are really looking forward to what Christmas has to offer. For many Cancerians the festive season starts right now and you will be getting into the right frame of mind. Keep an eye on a family member who might have been out of sorts recently.

18 WEDNESDAY — *Moon Age Day 22   Moon Sign Aries*

You seem to have lots of ideas at your disposal. Even if eight out of ten of them are not workable, that still leaves two that are worth pursuing. With only a few days left until Christmas actually begins, your mind tends to travel back to previous times. There are lessons to be learned from the past but probably not many.

19 THURSDAY — *Moon Age Day 23   Moon Sign Taurus*

A friendly word in the right ear might make it easy for you to settle a personal issue that has been on your mind. At the same time you can be of significant assistance to colleagues, friends and your partner. The Crab is presently at its most co-operative, which enhances your natural popularity.

20 FRIDAY
Moon Age Day 24   Moon Sign Taurus

As the holidays approach you get more and more from social situations and gatherings in general. The attitude of family members can be variable but you do need to express your own opinions frankly. There is no point whatsoever in leaving people guessing and the truthful path is the right one every time this week.

21 SATURDAY
Moon Age Day 25   Moon Sign Gemini

There is now a good chance to improve your mind in some way, as well as to learn that you are in any case smarter than you might have thought. You love to pit your wits against those of interesting people, whilst at the same time showing the distinctly competitive edge of your Crab nature.

22 SUNDAY
Moon Age Day 26   Moon Sign Gemini

Daily life might be subject to sudden change and that could mean having to think on your feet a good deal today. Although you would be comfortable at home, it's possible you will take time out to visit relatives and the change of scenery could work to your advantage.

23 MONDAY
Moon Age Day 27   Moon Sign Cancer

This is a good time for communicating with others in any way. If you are at work, you may forge a special bond will colleagues; if not, enjoy a chat with friends. Don't let the winter weather keep you inside because it's clear that you need some fresh air in your lungs. Those Cancerians who are already away for Christmas may benefit the most.

24 TUESDAY
Moon Age Day 28   Moon Sign Cancer

There may be some very hopeful news with regard to your personal concerns and wishes on this Christmas Eve. From a social and romantic point of view, it is those things that come like a bolt from the blue that offer the most, so don't be either upset or worried if you have to change your attitude or plans at the last minute.

25 WEDNESDAY   *Moon Age Day 29   Moon Sign Leo*

Christmas Day is likely to find you in the company of family members. You are especially drawn to younger people at present, not simply because of the season but on account of a number of planetary influences that surround you now. It is possible to feel very warm and content throughout most of today.

26 THURSDAY   *Moon Age Day 0   Moon Sign Leo*

Certain situations just won't work out the way you want them to and there isn't very much you can do about it. The lunar low has come around so this is a very good day for simply going with the flow. If you try to do too much there's a good chance that much of it will have to be done again at a later date.

27 FRIDAY   *Moon Age Day 1   Moon Sign Virgo*

The temporary lull does at least give you the chance to look at situations without rushing into them. You will also have more time for loved ones and to pay attention to your partner. If there is someone you haven't seen for a while, call round and have a lengthy chat. It could cheer them up no end.

28 SATURDAY   *Moon Age Day 2   Moon Sign Virgo*

You should be in the market for a fairly satisfying sort of day, even if you discover that not everyone has been telling the truth of late. There are also trends pointing to some fairly unconventional behaviour by relatives or even close friends. Whatever happens, don't show that you are shocked.

29 SUNDAY   *Moon Age Day 3   Moon Sign Libra*

Family gatherings ought to be of real interest now and you will be doing more than most to make these possible. Even if you do not come from a very close family background you are likely to feel more attached than usual. A sense of place and belonging is extremely important to you at present.

30 MONDAY
Moon Age Day 4   Moon Sign Libra

This is a good time during which to try your hand at money making and innovative enterprises. Help with these is certain if you ask around as people generally seem to want to assist you today. There is a quieter side to your mood that shows later but in the main you should be happy to be in the social mainstream.

31 TUESDAY
Moon Age Day 5   Moon Sign Libra

Try to go with the flow where New Year parties are concerned and don't insist on making all the arrangements yourself, but also don't forget to get in touch with people who are living far away. Beware the possibility of unintentionally upsetting someone you care for, think before you speak, and all will be well.

RISING SIGNS FOR CANCER

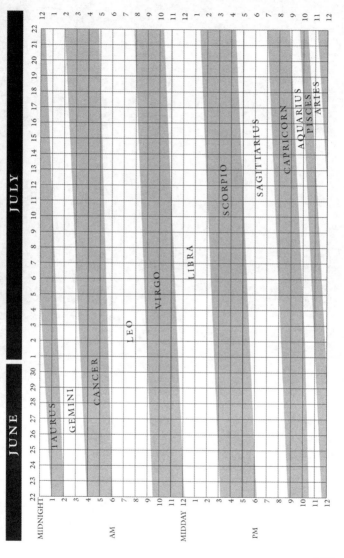

157

THE ZODIAC, PLANETS AND CORRESPONDENCES

The Earth revolves around the Sun once every calendar year, so when viewed from Earth the Sun appears in a different part of the sky as the year progresses. In astrology, these parts of the sky are divided into the signs of the zodiac and this means that the signs are organised in a circle. The circle begins with the sign of Aries and ends with Pisces.

Taking the zodiac sign as a starting point, astrologers then work with all the positions of planets, stars and many other factors to calculate horoscopes and birth charts and tell us what the stars have in store for us.

The table below shows the planets and Elements for each of the signs of the zodiac. Each sign belongs to one of the four Elements: Fire, Air, Earth or Water. Fire signs are creative and enthusiastic; Air signs are mentally active and thoughtful; Earth signs are constructive and practical; Water signs are emotional and have strong feelings.

It also shows the metals and gemstones associated with, or corresponding with, each sign. The correspondence is made when a metal or stone possesses properties that are held in common with a particular sign of the zodiac.

Finally, the table shows the opposite of each star sign – this is the opposite sign in the astrological circle.

Placed	Sign	Symbol	Element	Planet	Metal	Stone	Opposite
1	Aries	Ram	Fire	Mars	Iron	Bloodstone	Libra
2	Taurus	Bull	Earth	Venus	Copper	Sapphire	Scorpio
3	Gemini	Twins	Air	Mercury	Mercury	Tiger's Eye	Sagittarius
4	Cancer	Crab	Water	Moon	Silver	Pearl	Capricorn
5	Leo	Lion	Fire	Sun	Gold	Ruby	Aquarius
6	Virgo	Maiden	Earth	Mercury	Mercury	Sardonyx	Pisces
7	Libra	Scales	Air	Venus	Copper	Sapphire	Aries
8	Scorpio	Scorpion	Water	Pluto	Plutonium	Jasper	Taurus
9	Sagittarius	Archer	Fire	Jupiter	Tin	Topaz	Gemini
10	Capricorn	Goat	Earth	Saturn	Lead	Black Onyx	Cancer
11	Aquarius	Waterbearer	Air	Uranus	Uranium	Amethyst	Leo
12	Pisces	Fishes	Water	Neptune	Tin	Moonstone	Virgo